"*The Myth of Equality* is written so skillfully that it's easy to miss how much it accomplishes. The first part brings to light, with unflinching honesty, how deeply racism and white privilege are embedded within the founding documents and practices of the United States. The second part masterfully shows that this inequality violates the call of the gospel to justice and unity. And the third part offers some wise suggestions to those of us who are white Christians about how we can 'lay down' our white privilege. I have no doubt that some readers will be angered by the claim that they participate in and benefit from structures of racism and white privilege, well supported though that claim is. I predict that there will be more who are convinced and inspired by the patient, passionate, and nondefensive way in which Wytsma makes his case. It's a book that someone had to write."

Nicholas Wolterstorff, Noah Porter Professor Emeritus of Philosophical Theology, Yale University, senior research fellow, Institute for Advanced Studies in Culture, University of Virginia, honorary professor, Australian Catholic University

"White progressives, evangelical and not, seem to enjoy feeling bad about racial injustice and wagging self-righteous fingers at others, but they often exacerbate the injustices of racism by hardening the lines of defense. Far too often the only solutions proposed are more laws, tightening existing laws, and social engineering through public education. What we need are not resolutions but solutions—solutions emerging from real people in real settings, with leaders who have discovered the long, painful path that leads from white privilege and white invisibility to social integration, racial reconciliation, and churches abounding in fellowship across racial lines and celebrating the glories of ethnicities. Ken Wytsma is the kind of leader who offers real solutions toward social integration and racial reconciliation, and he comes from that kind of community and church. *The Myth of Equality* is a genuine contribution for those of us looking for ways forward."

Scot McKnight, Julius R. Mantey Professor of New Testament, Northern Seminary

"Ken Wytsma is a white evangelical man from a conservative white evangelical world, and he is doing his homework on race. I've witnessed Ken's journey toward deeper understanding of the construct of race, its impact on individuals and communities of color, and what redemption requires. I've witnessed the wrestling and the transformation as *aha* moments have moved him into deeper love, more solid commitment, and earnest work toward the healing of our world. Through *The Myth of Equality*, Wytsma offers a peek at his homework. But this is no cheat sheet. It's a journal of discoveries shared with humility, grace, and unrelenting commitment to truth."

Lisa Sharon Harper, chief church engagement officer, Sojourners, author of *The Very Good Gospel*

"With great sensitivity, wisdom, and boldness, Ken takes on the tough, often-taboo topics of privilege and race. He makes a cogent, powerful, and compelling argument for why addressing race and understanding privilege allows us to more fully live out the gospel. He boils down complicated concepts to relatable points through his interweaving of scholars' writings, activists' thinking, historical realities, and personal stories. His humility and posture of learning from others, particularly people of color, make this book an authentic, effective tool for followers of Christ taking seriously the call to pursue justice. This book is needed, timely, and will help reshape the conversation around race in America."

Jenny Yang, vice president of advocacy and policy, World Relief

"This book is truly amazing! Ken tackles the essentials of a major issue of our times with humility, honesty, intellect, and vulnerability. The result is a terrible beauty, a true invitation to come to terms with our own capacity for harm and good—leading us toward change and the hope of a generation reconciled. If you are perplexed about racial tension in this country, read this book. If you are worried about your complicity because of the color of your skin, read this book. If you feel ill equipped to speak about this issue, read this book. If you aren't sure what your faith requires of you in this space, read this book. Honestly, read this book. It's important."

Danielle Strickland, social justice secretary, The Salvation Army, USW

"We must know our past to understand our present. Racial injustice in America's history has constructed massive systemic challenges we face today. To move forward well, we need a variety of voices—especially minority voices. The conversation is further strengthened by white voices willing to own the privilege this history affords rather than ignore or deny it. In the pages that follow, Wytsma, a respected Christian leader in the justice conversation, gives a strong introduction to our country's brutal history with race, confronting the 'myth of equality' in America, joining a multiethnic chorus of voices grappling honestly and prophetically with how to best move forward."

Joshua Ryan Butler, author of *The Skeletons in God's Closet* and *The Pursuing God*

"It is impossible to deny that Christ is moving his church today toward racial reconciliation. It is likewise impossible to deny that many white Christians like me are not as comfortable with that movement as we say we are. In *The Myth of Equality*, Ken engages a visceral topic with clarity, compassion, and inspiring conviction. He prompts us to engage the deep and bitter roots of racial bias and privilege in American faith. A must-read resource for those beginning to feel that 'the way things are' is not okay. A readable, well-reasoned push toward Christ's justice."

Paul J. Pastor, author of *The Face of the Deep*

"White privilege is a subject that few dare to tackle. I applaud Ken for venturing into this rough terrain. Ken's historical approach to white privilege drives the conversation deeper and challenges readers to move beyond a political perspective, toward a kingdom view. His personal journey keeps it grounded in reality. A much needed book for our times."

Leroy Barber, The Voices Project

"Ken Wytsma goes where few dare to tread. He asks hard questions about race, justice, and equality and presents proven and practical solutions. Above all, Ken personifies these solutions; he is seeking to live justice, not just do it. The message in *The Myth of Equality* is urgent; it's a must-read."

Stephan Bauman, former president and CEO of World Relief, author of *Break Open the Sky*

"These are challenging times in our larger culture—and within the church. In the midst of these tensions, I'm grateful for voices like Ken Wytsma who are seeking to help the church not only to engage the various challenges but to do it from a posture of humility and deep self-reflection. In *The Myth of Equality*, Wytsma broaches an incredibly sensitive but pertinent conversation about equality, privilege, race, injustice, and reconciliation. But herein lies the challenge: many of us love the idea of reconciliation—until we learn that it inevitably involves the messy and arduous work of listening to others' stories, truth telling, confessing, repenting, dismantling, healing, and peacemaking. *The Myth of Equality* is an important and timely book that helps us dig deeper on the journey of justice and reconciliation."

Eugene Cho, pastor and humanitarian, author of *Overrated*

"This is an important and courageous book. At this moment of national tension around racial questions, Ken Wytsma stakes out unique territory, building the bridges necessary for many white evangelicals to grasp the core of the issue and become faithful brothers and sisters to Christians of color. I am thankful for his hard work and fearless dedication to justice."

Alexia Salvatierra, coauthor of *Faith-Rooted Organizing*

"*The Myth of Equality* is a book for our times. Tumultuous times do not create problems, they reveal them. Political disruption, racial division, and extreme polarization mandate that the church looks itself in the mirror. We must recognize that to whom much is given, much is expected. Privilege is not just a modern progressive agenda, it is an ancient, biblically recognized reality. Ken Wytsma has done the church a favor that can help us recapture the blessed virtue of giving. Leaders seriously interested in helping Christians navigate these important issues would be well served to engage this book."

Tyler Johnson, lead pastor, Redemption Arizona

"One of the greatest obstacles to the journey toward racial justice and reconciliation within the US church is the refusal of white Christians to confront the realities of white supremacy and white privilege. Here, Ken Wytsma comes alongside white Christians to help them tackle this issue, not from the perspective of a distant expert, but as one who continues to wrestle with how privilege and racism impact his own discipleship journey. Rooted in Scripture, history, and personal experience, *The Myth of Equality* is a valuable primer for anyone struggling to understand racism and privilege."

Chanequa Walker-Barnes, associate professor of practical theology, McAfee School of Theology, Mercer University, author of *Too Heavy a Yoke*

"Racism. Immigration. White supremacy. Privilege. We hear these words on the news and we see them thrown around on Facebook, but the reality is that most of us white evangelicals have a shallow understanding of their meanings, their origins, and their deep roots in our country. This is exactly why we need Ken Wytsma's brave and informative new book *The Myth of Equality* so that we may have a better understanding of our past and present and begin to truly engage in the difficult work of true reconciliation."

Lindsey Nobles, chief operating officer and strategist, IF:Gathering

"Stretching back to the earliest arrivals of Europeans on our coasts, the United States has been built on a long history of racial and ethnic injustice, and white Christians have been strikingly reticent about this history. Ken Wytsma's *The Myth of Equality* gently and gracefully initiates a conversation with white Christians about the racial brokenness of our land. This is a timely book that speaks bluntly about our past and in so doing orients us for the long, slow journey toward healing these wounds."

C. Christopher Smith, founding editor of *The Englewood Review of Books*, author of *Reading For the Common Good*

"The American church stands at an important crossroads. Will we embrace God's plan for the church as revealed in Revelation 7:9, or will the church disintegrate into the chaos, confusion, and cacophony akin to the story of the Tower of Babel as we build dividing walls of hostility? In order to move into God's heart for the church, truth telling must occur. Without truth, we simply rebuild the Tower of Babel rather than become the people of God. In this book, Ken Wytsma embraces the courage needed to speak the truth in love. Wytsma speaks the truth even at the risk of putting himself in peril. That kind of truth telling is much needed in our turbulent world. Thank you, Ken, for the courage expressed in this book. May you who engage this book also find the similar courage to take these truths and be transformed by them."

Soong-Chan Rah, Milton B. Engebretson Professor of Church Growth and Evangelism, North Park Theological Seminary, author of *The Next Evangelicalism* and *Prophetic Lament*

THE
MYTH
OF
EQUALITY

Uncovering the Roots
of Injustice and Privilege

KEN WYTSMA

IVP Books

An imprint of InterVarsity Press
Downers Grove, Illinois

InterVarsity Press
P.O. Box 1400, Downers Grove, IL 60515-1426
ivpress.com
email@ivpress.com

InterVarsity Press® is the book-publishing division of InterVarsity Christian Fellowship/USA®, a movement of students and faculty active on campus at hundreds of universities, colleges, and schools of nursing in the United States of America, and a member movement of the International Fellowship of Evangelical Students. For information about local and regional activities, visit intervarsity.org.

All Scripture quotations, unless otherwise indicated, are taken from THE HOLY BIBLE, NEW INTERNATIONAL VERSION®, NIV® Copyright © 1973, 1978, 1984, 2011 by Biblica, Inc.™ Used by permission. All rights reserved worldwide.

While any stories in this book are true, some names and identifying information may have been changed to protect the privacy of individuals.

Figure 1: Untitled, Harlem, New York, 1947. Photographs by Gordon Parks. Courtesy of and copyright The Gordon Parks Foundation.

Figure 4: 1938 Federal Housing Administration map. Public domain.

Figure 5: Image copyright 2013, Weldon Cooper Center for Public Service, Rector and Visitors of the University of Virginia (Dustin A. Cable, creator). Map data by OpenStreetMap. © OpenStreetMap contributors, under CC–BY–SA.

Cover design: David Fassett
Interior design: Daniel van Loon
Author photo: Benjamin Edwards Photography

ISBN 978-0-8308-4482-1 (print)
ISBN 978-0-8308-8108-6 (digital)

Printed in the United States of America ∞

Library of Congress Cataloging-in-Publication Data
Names: Wytsma, Ken, author.
Title: The myth of equality : uncovering the roots of injustice and privilege
  / Ken Wytsma.
Description: Downers Grove : InterVarsity Press, 2017. | Includes
  bibliographical references.
Identifiers: LCCN 2017000166 (print) | LCCN 2017008460 (ebook) | ISBN
  9780830844821 (casebound : alk. paper) | ISBN 9780830881086 (eBook)
Subjects: LCSH: Christianity and justice. | Racism--United States. | United
  States--Race relations. | Equality--Religious aspects--Christianity.
Classification: LCC BR115.J8 W975 2017 (print) | LCC BR115.J8 (ebook) | DDC
  261.80973--dc23
LC record available at https://lccn.loc.gov/2017000166

P 21 20 19 18 17 16 15 14 13 12 11 10 9 8 7 6 5 4 3 2 1
Y 35 34 33 32 31 30 29 28 27 26 25 24 23 22 21 20 19 18 17

To live under the American Constitution is the greatest political privilege that was ever accorded to the human race.

CALVIN COOLIDGE

Representatives and direct Taxes shall be apportioned among the several States which may be included within this Union, according to their respective Numbers, which shall be determined by adding to the whole Number of free Persons, including those bound to Service for a Term of Years, and *excluding Indians* not taxed, *three fifths of all other Persons*.

UNITED STATES CONSTITUTION,
ARTICLE I, SECTION 2, CLAUSE 3 (EMPHASIS ADDED)

TO

Donna and Leroy Barber
Juanita and Rudy Rasmus
Joy and David Bailey

*For late-night conversations
in some beautiful places.*

CONTENTS

Introduction   1

PART I | THE STORY OF RACE

1 America's White Standard:
A Nation of (European) Immigrants   11

2 When the World Became Racist:
Color in the Western Tradition   29

3 Stolen Labor   47

4 How Our Cities Got Their Shape:
The Great Migration, Redlining, and the
Roots of Modern Segregation   67

PART II | EQUALITY AND THE KINGDOM OF GOD

5 The Aristocratic Itch   85

6 Does Justice Belong in Our Gospel Conversation?   101

7 The Salvation Industrial Complex   117

8 A Short Look at American Individualism   129

PART III | THE CHALLENGE OF PRIVILEGE

9 When Racism Went Underground:
Implicit Racial Bias and the Stories That Hide Within Us   137

10 The Voice of Justice   153

11 Finding Ourselves in the Other   167

Conclusion   185

Acknowledgments   193

Appendix: Recommended Reading   195

Notes   199

Index   213

If God made this world, why should it be a surprise that the things we believe about God connect us to the world he made?

VINCENT BACOTE, PROFESSOR OF THEOLOGY, WHEATON COLLEGE

INTRODUCTION

The opposite of love is not hate, it's indifference.

The opposite of art is not ugliness, it's indifference.

The opposite of faith is not heresy, it's indifference.

And the opposite of life is not death, it's indifference.

ELIE WIESEL

I WAS ATTENDING a Christian Community Development Association (CCDA) conference in New Orleans when a friend of mine, who was beginning an urban church plant in south-central Los Angeles, asked if I could meet with his leadership team.

This friend is African American, with a long history of community development work, so I was surprised when he requested the meeting. He asked specifically that I talk about justice with the younger white copastors helping him with the church plant.

Surely there's nothing I could add to that conversation that he wouldn't already know, I thought.

We met for lunch on the second day of the conference in the large atrium restaurant on the first floor. The midday sun was shining through to our table, and hundreds of conferencegoers were milling about the atrium. For quite a while our little group just caught up, discussed ministry, and enjoyed our food.

After some time, one of the young white pastors began to get animated as he told us about a new relationship he was developing in the urban neighborhood of the church plant.

He had befriended a young black man in his twenties. They had been spending a lot of time together, and the young pastor was excited about their growing friendship but really frustrated at something the young man had recently said.

"You'll never fully get it," the young African American had stated bluntly on matters of race. "No matter how hard you try, it *won't* be the same for you and you *can't* fully understand."

This comment didn't surprise me, but the pastor's reaction did.

"I can't stand this reverse-racism stuff," he declared with an air of indignation. "It's so not fair for him to put me in a box and say just because I'm white that I'll never get it and can't fully understand what he does."

It was then I realized why my friend had asked me to lunch. There were things that I, as an educated white man, could say about white privilege and blind spots that he never could.

I spent the next half-hour explaining that experiences of not being treated preferentially and of being told you'll never truly understand the first-person experience of being discriminated against are far different from experiencing racism.

Racism is the diminishment of worth in men and women in and through bias, systems, and power structures that disadvantage them in tangible ways based on skin color.

Reverse racism is a phrase thrown around when white people are singled out or described in terms of their whiteness. It is often, however, a gross misapplication of the idea of racism.

This is important, as many people, not fully comprehending the nature of true racism, want to push back by asserting reverse racism or prejudice against whites.

This pastor, just because he has noble intentions of ministering in an urban neighborhood, isn't entitled to think he can truly know someone else's experience. Further, the white pastor isn't being marginalized or disadvantaged—not economically, not physically, not structurally—when a young black man tells him that his efforts aren't enough to make him fully understand the effects of racism.

Regard is something we all crave. In fact, preferential treatment is something most humans enjoy. This has been the reality and legacy for many whites in America. In many respects, however, the preferential treatment of whites is in decline. What isn't in question is that the United States is becoming multicultural, and by the mid-2040s, for the first time, it will be over 50 percent black and brown.[1]

Losing preferential treatment or letting go of privilege, which the young pastor above was struggling with, is not the same as experiencing oppression when institutionalized systems and structures harm someone on the basis of the color of their skin.

Not having as much of a voice as we whites are used to can be jarring, but it's not the same as suffering racism.

HOW THIS STORY BEGAN

I was asked to write *The Myth of Equality*.

I was approached with the idea for this book by Helen Lee, from InterVarsity Press (IVP), after a lecture on privilege during a June 2015 conference. I didn't immediately say yes.

The idea of such a book had been on IVP's table for some time. They wanted to publish a book on race and privilege, written by a white evangelical, that could serve as a bridge between those at the forefront of race relations in America and the many Americans and evangelicals beginning to awaken to our racist history—a book that asks deeper questions about race, identity, and responsibility.

As it happened, two events on the weekend of the conference accelerated my decision. The first was when a major hotel in Chicago racially profiled some of the conference attendees and hotel guests.[2]

The second occured the following morning, the final day of the conference, when the videotape of a white police officer breaking up a midday pool party in McKinney, Texas, and violently manhandling and humiliating a black teenage girl came to national attention.

The officer, singling out African American youth while ignoring white teenagers, violently wrestled to the ground the unarmed girl, who wore only a bathing suit. He quickly placed all his weight on her, digging his knee into her spine. He stayed fixed in this position for minutes as she sobbed and as her young friends and some grown men begged him to get off her back.

I'm sure this is a standard technique that police officers are trained to use, but it was obvious to anyone watching this video that what he was doing was unnecessary, abusive, and deeply traumatizing. It broke the hearts of all who saw it. I'm a father of four girls, and nothing pains my heart more deeply than seeing the dignity of any girl trampled on, especially by someone in a position of authority who is observably out of control.

For these reasons—even before reaching out to my network of friends to get their advice—I knew that I would write this book. Some topics we choose. Some choose us.

It's a difficult topic, however. How do we care about race without swinging to an extreme reaction such as blaming all cops because of the actions of some? Or how do we find it in ourselves to recognize our racial privilege even when our business is going bankrupt, we're working ourselves to the bone, and don't feel very privileged?

I do not think I'm the enlightened white guy who "gets it," and I don't believe there are simple answers to fix the race problems in America. This is not a subject easily broached. It is complicated, deeply personal, and colored by politics and religion.

It is also a costly conversation. And the truth is, we all love justice, until there's a cost.

Racial bias is a subject with many subtleties. Issues of race go deeper than we often realize.

In a recent Barna survey, only 56 percent of evangelicals agree that people of color are often placed at a social disadvantage, *lower* than the national average of 67 percent. At the same time, 95 percent of evangelicals think the church plays a critical role in racial reconciliation—*higher* than the national average of 73 percent. Taken together, these findings reveal that those who believe they are most equipped to help with reconciliation actually don't think it is needed as much as other Americans do.[3]

Race is a topic that evangelicals are often willing to dismiss despite recognizing we have something to contribute. As one writer notes, "The irony of American history is the tendency of good white Americans to presume racial innocence. Ignorance of how we are shaped racially is the first sign of privilege. In other words, it is a privilege to ignore the consequences of race in America."[4] Or, as Rev. Traci Blackmon so aptly put it in her November 9, 2015, tweet: "Endless dialogue is a tool of the privileged."

Are evangelicals susceptible to neglect the realities of racism?

Maybe.

PRIVILEGE AND RESPONSIBILITY

After summarizing the findings of the Barna study cited above (Barna is a Christian research group), researcher Brooke Hempell draws a conclusion that should give us great pause: "More than any other segment of the population, white evangelical Christians demonstrate a blindness to the struggle of their African American brothers and sisters." She continues, "This is a dangerous reality for the modern church."[5]

Hempell's conclusion matches my experience. I've spent most of my life in a middle-class white evangelical culture. I went to a well-regarded conservative seminary, and I have worked in conservative churches for the past twenty-five years. For the most part, in my experience, issues of race have been viewed (1) as being behind us, (2) as something that will be fixed when others take up more responsibility, or (3) as being mired in leftist political agendas that conservatives must stoutly oppose.

What I hadn't experienced until recently was evangelicals choosing to take a different vantage point, seeking to fully grapple with the reality of racism in American history, to humanize the experience of minorities; to understand what privilege and responsibility might look like—not for others, but for Christ followers in the majority culture.

Privilege and responsibility—these are the two themes of this book.

I'm hoping that this book can serve as an introduction for people who feel that something is wrong, are looking for a way to understand the roots of racism in America, or are looking for language to make sense of their experience.

I am not attempting to be the authoritative voice on race in America, and I can only really speak from a perspective of privilege and my experience. I am simply addressing a topic to which Scripture speaks clearly, a reality that in many ways has helped to shape my story. Indeed it has played a significant role in shaping the stories of all Americans, whether we know it or not. Speaking only to safe topics, where agreement comes easily, can't be the chief goal of faithful witness. It wasn't for Jesus.

The central thesis of this book is that a misunderstanding of the gospel leads to a false dichotomy: we prioritize the spiritual and personal aspects of faith and devalue or nullify the material and communal dimensions that bind us to God's creation and to our brothers and sisters made in the image of God. This twisting of faith has resulted in historic injustices that have terrorized and handicapped generations of minorities. The result today is a society where we are deeply shaped by racial categories, yet we who are white remain mostly blind to how the undercurrent of racialized thinking affects our life as a nation and our own actions.

Put another way, racism in the United States is worse than we thought, its lasting consequences are more significant than we think, and our responsibility is greater than we've been taught. And that is the order in which I have structured the argument of this book. If, however, you are not at all sure that racism should be a central concern of our Christian spirituality and a primary conversation in our churches, you might want to start by reading part two, and then read parts one and three.

Maya Angelou once wrote, "All great artists draw from the same resource: the human heart, which tells us that we are all more alike than we are unalike."[6]

As we explore this topic together, may we come to know ourselves better, see God more clearly, and find ourselves growing in solidarity with one another.

PART I

THE STORY
OF RACE

ONE

AMERICA'S WHITE STANDARD

A Nation of (European) Immigrants

> Lift every voice and sing,
> Till earth and heaven ring,
> Ring with the harmonies of Liberty;
> Let our rejoicing rise
> High as the list'ning skies,
> Let it resound loud as the rolling sea.
> Sing a song full of the faith that the dark past has taught us,
> Sing a song full of the hope that the present has brought us;
> Facing the rising sun of our new day begun,
> Let us march on till victory is won.
>
> **JAMES WELDON JOHNSON** (1871-1938),
> "LIFT EVERY VOICE AND SING"

IN HIS RECENT BOOK and documentary *America: Imagine the World Without Her*, conservative author Dinesh D'Souza argues persuasively, but dangerously, that the progressive political agenda is tantamount to trying to "shame" America rather than recognizing and admitting her strengths.

I acknowledge the many strengths of the United States that D'Souza points out, and I certainly find some of his language of American exceptionalism compelling. But I disagree with D'Souza on the oversimplified dichotomy that we are either praising America or shaming her.

There is a difference between shaming and truth telling. The former is for the purpose of tearing down without the goal of building up. The purposes of truth telling, on the other hand, range from a disinterested pursuit of facts to an honest facing of history and culture in pursuit of a more just future.

There's an old saying addressed to those who are hunting for a church: if you find a perfect church, don't join or you will mess it up. People are imperfect and messy, so we should expect congregations made up of people to be messy too.

I think this holds at a national level as well. People are imperfect and messy (the theological language would be that we all have a propensity for sin), and so we should expect our country, made up of sinful people, to be messy too. One look at Congress and its language, rancor, and antics should be enough to convince people that we're far from perfect. The fact that the United States has 4.4 percent of the world's population but 22.2 percent of the world's incarcerated men and women might also show that we're far from our best selves.[1]

What I think D'Souza misses is that America really is an organism (note that he refers to it as "her" in his movie title) and that it is perfectly legitimate to take a critical look without shaming. I visit my doctor each year for checkups on my well-being. With every passing year there seem to be more and more things to be checked and evaluated. Knowing the truth of my physical state allows me to get and stay healthy. And every doctor I visit wants a full medical history (the truth about my life up until that point) so they can best diagnose my current condition and best prescribe future treatment.

My desire in looking at our racial past (what has been called "America's Original Sin" in the late twentieth century)[2] isn't to push America down but to help us know our medical history, as it were, so we can better prescribe the kinds of attitudes and behaviors that might help us repent, turn from our sin, and find reconciliation.

A NATION OF IMMIGRANTS

Though we romanticize historic immigration and like to boast that we are a nation of immigrants, from the beginning not all races were created equal in America's immigration and naturalization policies.

I often hear news pundits or see social media posts claiming that although America has a checkered past, we have progressed so far beyond our past mistakes that it is time for minorities to move on—to "get over it." People making claims like this fail to realize that when a tragedy such as the slave trade or segregation in the South occurs, there are long historical aftershocks. Slavery and segregation may have been dismantled, but racism remains built into our society, and its effects will last for generations.

In order to understand the current state of race relations in the United States, we have to study how they developed.

Among the original Western European colonists and founders of our country, British sentiments and preferences prevailed. In a pamphlet written in 1751, Benjamin Franklin wrote, "Why should Pennsylvania, founded by the English, become a Colony of Aliens who will shortly be so numerous as to Germanize us instead of our Anglifying them, and will never adopt our Language or Customs, any more than they can acquire our complexion?"[3] He goes on to say that there are actually very few "purely white people" in the world and identifies the English and Germans of Saxon descent as making up "the principal Body of White People on the Face of the Earth." Franklin admits his partiality for whites such as himself over those with "swarthier" and "tawnier" complexions, as well as the "Sons of Africa."[4] Such inclinations eventually settled into a general preference for whiteness that became based not just on skin color but how immigrants' way of life fit into the white American way of life.

In the early days of the United States, until after the Civil War, there were no laws *restricting* immigration. However, the Constitution of the United States gave Congress "the power to establish an uniform Rule of Naturalization," and in 1790 it took advantage of that power and established a naturalization act that allowed any "free white persons" who had been living in the United States for at least two years to become citizens.[5] Though anyone was free to enter the country, only whites who were not indentured servants were allowed to become citizens. This began a long social and legal process of defining whiteness.

In the early years of the law, it seems people were generally classified as white or nonwhite. However, in the late 1800s, more people began to enter the United States who did not fit the socially accepted racial categories. John Tehranian, law professor at Southwestern University, notes that between 1878 and 1952, fifty-two individuals sued to be declared white after immigration officials denied their citizenship request on the grounds of "racial ineligibility."[6]

According to Tehranian, the legal definition of "whiteness" was important not only for citizenship but for other rights such as property ownership. For example, in California the Alien Land Law—passed in 1920 and affirmed as constitutional by the US Supreme Court—prohibited noncitizens from owning land. So at that point only whites, Americans of African descent (former slaves), and those who went to court and could convince a judge to rule on their "whiteness" had legal rights to own property and participate fully in the economy.[7]

From these cases and legal debates, Tehranian argues that the law contributed strongly to the social construct of race. About this period he writes,

> The dominant criterion for the determination of whiteness was not a scientific standard or even a common-knowledge test. . . . Instead, whiteness was determined through performance. . . . [People] demonstrated evidence of whiteness in their character, religious practices and beliefs, class orientation, language, ability to intermarry, and a host of other traits that had nothing to do with intrinsic racial grouping.[8]

Immigrants whom "judges saw as most fit to carry on the tradition of the 'White Republic'" were deemed white and allowed to become citizens and own property. In summary, "white privilege became a quid pro quo for white performance."[9]

After the Naturalization Act of 1790, racial inclusion in the immigration and naturalization process proceeded in fits and starts. On February 2, 1848, the United States and Mexico signed the Treaty of Guadalupe Hidalgo. This treaty ended the Mexican-American War and added half of modern-day California, Nevada, and Utah, and parts of Colorado, Arizona, Wyoming, and New Mexico to the territory of the United States—along with nearly one hundred thousand Mexicans, who automatically became US citizens.[10]

The Naturalization Act of 1870 introduced policies and punishments for fraudulent practices but also expanded the naturalization process to include those of "African nativity and to persons of African descent." However, at this time there were still many other nonwhites who had immigrated to the United States and were unable to become citizens—most notably, Chinese.[11]

According to census data, by 1870 there were sixty thousand Chinese in the United States, many who immigrated during the Gold Rush and others who came later looking for employment in constructing the Union Pacific and Central Pacific Railroads.[12] In *Welcoming the Stranger*, Matthew Soerens and Jenny Hwang Yang—Christian activists and experts on American immigration policy—explain: "As has proven to be a theme throughout American history with immigrants from throughout the world, though, the Chinese were welcomed when their labor was needed, but once work became scarce, the welcome wore thin."[13] Once the railroads were completed with the aid of Chinese laborers, public opinion shifted: the Chinese were treated as racially inferior and subjected to a series of ordinances and laws designed to drive them out and stop them from taking jobs from US citizens. Historians also documented cases of Chinese being "forcibly driven from

their homes and . . . in other cases victims of lynching and other violence."[14] As the anti-Chinese hysteria continued, there were calls to
stop immigration from China altogether. In 1882 the Chinese Exclusion Act was passed—"the first significant federal legislation lim-
iting immigration."[15] The law was repealed in 1943, at which time
foreign-born Chinese became eligible for naturalization.

Racial exclusion was a staple of US immigration policy until the
McCarran-Walter Act of 1952, which eliminated race as a basis for
exclusion, but other discriminatory practices existed until 1965.[16]

Did you catch that? Until 1952 you had to be white, deemed white
by a court, born on American soil, or of African American descent to
be afforded the *full* rights of an American citizen of the United States.
This sounds crazy to me, and for much of my life I wasn't aware of it,
even though I grew up conscious of immigration issues. In fact, it was
just one year after the racial factors were eliminated from immigration
laws that my dad and his family arrived by boat as immigrants from
Holland. It was less than a decade after World War II ended and just
before oil was found in the North Sea, which revitalized the econ-
omies of both England and Holland.

MY FAMILY'S IMMIGRATION STORY

I always knew my dad was an immigrant (we have a particularly Dutch
name, we celebrated Dutch traditions such as St. Nicholas Day, and we
ate Dutch pastries on New Year's Eve), but my dad never really talked
much about it. In recent years he's opened up a lot more, talking about
growing up during the destruction along the coast of Holland—
particularly Rotterdam—and how his family got a new start in Pas-
adena, California. The Dutch government paid for their boat tickets and
gave them a stipend for a household shipment, but they weren't allowed
to leave the country with more than the equivalent of twenty US dollars
in their pockets. Apparently my grandpa thought about cheating and
rolling bills into gauze but, with my dad watching, decided against it.

Nobody in our family spoke English, and my dad remembers how, as a new immigrant to California at age eight, he really was the odd man out. "Kids can be cruel," he said; "they pick on anyone who is different." My dad's family endured many challenges: my grandmother was wheelchair-bound with multiple sclerosis, and my grandfather worked several jobs to make ends meet. But through it all, he was able to be part of the great "melting pot" that was the new America. I can never remember a time when he spoke with anything other than an American accent or that he ever had trouble fitting in at a social gathering.

For me, and for much of his life, my dad was fully American. The GI Bill paid for his advanced degree, and after marrying my mom, he had a very successful career in the United States Navy, retiring as a captain in command of reservists at Norfolk, Virginia.

My family's story reveals how the idea of a melting pot reflected reality. You could truly immigrate, learn the language, and blend in at that time. The melting-pot ideal didn't mean that all different races melted together; however, it meant that *European* ethnicities could be melded into one normative American society. This idea didn't gain currency until after World War II when Americans had a paternalistic view toward much of Europe because of the war efforts.

Later in life, when my dad was in his sixties working in leadership at a company after retiring from the Navy, one of his colleagues was a friend of Korean descent named Sam. Sam immigrated to the United States as an eight-year-old—the same age my dad was when his family arrived—and also in the mid-1950s, but he spoke with a very distinctive Korean accent. What made the difference? Based on a conversation they had, my dad says it was because nearly all of Sam's social interactions were in the Korean community, whereas my dad spent all of his time in an English-speaking community.

When I asked my dad if this was related to color, he said, "If you don't fit in physically or culturally, it forces small communities of immigrants to become tighter and to stay stronger." Maybe if my dad had been a different color, it would have been harder to blend in. Or maybe if Sam's family had moved to an area that lacked a Korean community, he would have navigated language and culture differently. But in 1950s America, there was a very real sense in which the various nationalities of white Europe could melt into the pot, while others were less able to do so.[17]

Even though the McCarran-Walter Act of 1952 eliminated racist criteria from our immigration laws on paper, from 1924 to 1965 the United States had a quota system that restricted immigration based on nationality. In 1924 the initial law limited migration of a foreign population to no more than 2 percent of the population of each nationality already residing in the United States according to the 1890 census. The law used the 1890 census rather than the new 1920 census because the 1890 census had preceded the second great wave of immigrants; thus the new policy gave preference to immigrants from northern European countries and effectively excluded newer immigrants from other parts of Europe and Asia.[18] The exact percentages and census data used varied throughout the course of the quota system, but generally it served to limit immigrants who didn't fit the standards and preferences of white America. In the height of the civil rights movement, it was impossible to neglect racism in our immigration policy. Accordingly, the quota system was eliminated by reforms advocated by John F. Kennedy and finally passed by Lyndon Johnson in 1965. The reforms did away with the most explicitly racist immigration and naturalization policies, but we continue to wrestle with racial bias and other complicated immigration issues today.

Throughout our immigration history you can trace a pattern of how races or ethnicities were demonized and excluded. When we fear a certain group, we exclude them—and then, once we feel okay with that ethnic group, we demonize another.

As Christians we have a responsibility, when we see a pattern like this, to break the cycle of objectifying and marginalizing other people groups and defining ourselves as against and above them. If every person is made in the image of God, then stereotypes lead us down a dangerous path, short-circuiting the difficult process of loving our neighbors, even if they come from war-torn lands or from cultures completely unlike our own.

UNDERSTANDING WHITE SUPREMACY

People trying to understand race issues frequently ask about the phrase *white supremacy*. This phrase often comes up in conferences where speakers of color seek to advance deep conversation about the racial state of our society.

I remember sitting in the audience at The Justice Conference in Chicago in 2015, after a year of racial turmoil in the headlines. I was listening to a diverse group of speakers address racism, oppression, and racial tension. While black speakers felt comfortable using the phrase *white supremacy* and obviously believed that it described reality, the white speakers completely avoided it.

As I watched the white audience during the conference, scanned some of the social media feeds, and later read the emails that came to me after the conference, it became clear that many of the white leaders in the group were very uncomfortable with the language and even felt threatened or attacked by it.

The struggle for many white listeners is that they've only ever heard this phrase with regard to the Ku Klux Klan or other overtly racist people and organizations from our nation's past. So when they hear it now, they immediately tend to go on the defensive: "I'm not a white supremacist!"

White supremacy was most often used for the Klan and similar groups in the past, but it is increasingly used as a descriptive term in intellectual conversations around race in America today. It's important to understand how people are using language so we can enter more fully into the conversation, more to describe the framework of America than as an attack on a singular person. Here is how I tried to explain it to those who contacted me following The Justice Conference.

First, white supremacy in the United States is a historical fact. White supremacists, who held to preferential treatment of whites and a discriminatory view of people of color, ruled our government for much of our history. They enacted laws. They built systems. They created powerful social groups and pursued wealth in ways that cannot be fully separated from their racial views and racial policies.

This is "hard" white supremacy: the intentional building and maintaining of white power by those who did not or do not believe in equality.

Second, white supremacy is not only a historical fact; it is also a present reality. We see hard white supremacy today with modern-day fascists and others unabashedly arguing for the reestablishment of white control in America.

"Soft" white supremacy, on the other hand, is not about overt racists or acts of extreme prejudice. Rather, it is descriptive of what happened at the hands of white supremacists: a *white normative standard* that emerged throughout the history of our immigration system, as well as other policies, systems, and social structures. A white normative standard means that whiteness became and was ingrained as the bar or canon by which things were evaluated or contrasted. Whiteness became the racial category by which all others were evaluated.

This white normative standard (or the elevation and protection of whiteness) speaks to foundational aspects of our culture, both in its functioning and in its psychology. There are vestiges that remain, which means that achieving racial equality requires more than just obtaining forgiveness for past wrongs or diversifying our friend network. To be clear, soft white supremacy isn't just that we are riding a wave of consequence of something that predated us. It also speaks to a complicity in benefiting from racialized systems. The remains of white supremacy must be dismantled so that our society's foundations and social consciousness are no longer under the lingering shadow of a racialized white standard.

The phrase *white supremacy* is necessary if we are to have deep and nuanced conversations about our past, present, and future sins. White supremacy does not mean that white people are bad, that people of color are better, or that the only people responsible for societal ills are white. Defensiveness in response to the phrase *white supremacy* is an overreaction to a mature conversation. We must be prepared to listen rather than react.

White supremacy simply names a reality that was constructed brick by brick and, like ancient Roman ruins, still marks our landscape. Hard white supremacy would have never allowed a black president. Soft white supremacy is our current reality of racial profiling, mass incarceration of minorities, and a highly segregated society resulting from federal housing policies of previous generations—all while we had a black president.

Yes, we've had our first black president, and Harriet Tubman's image is now slated to appear on new twenty-dollar bills, but those are stitches of progress, not the complete fabric of equality we should be working toward.

The white standard or bias also speaks to the apparent success of Asian Americans in American society. Asian Americans have often been successful within white culture because they approximate it in many respects. When whites look at Asians and feel an affinity with them, it's often on the assumption that Asians seem able to mimic the Protestant work ethic and white values. But in actuality, they are likely embodying the values of *their own* culture. Many Asian cultures have long been known for their relational and communal values, their work ethic (in some cases born of Confucian thought), their focus on education, and other traits that are consonant with white Anglo-Saxon Protestant traditions.

So the fact that Asian Americans, compared with other cultural groups, are able to succeed in America still reflects racism when it is based on approximation to white majority culture rather than on a celebration and understanding of their own unique cultural values and contributions. Many have pointed to this phenomenon as the myth of the perfect immigrant, or the idea of the "model minority." This is complex; the white standard lies hidden in the ways that American society evaluates the "goodness" of various races.[19]

DIFFICULT CONVERSATIONS

What the conversation on white supremacy reveals for me is how hard we try to protect our comfort zone within the church. In what ways do our Christian cultures subtly develop, stagnate, and exclude conversations that would help us better understand each other and possibly grow to a greater unity?

A young chaplain of a Christian university recently asked me how to approach race from a Christian ministry and justice standpoint. He was wrestling with many of the same things I have wrestled with, and he asked if I would visit his school to speak on biblical justice. When I suggested that we make white privilege the topic instead of justice in general, his response was telling. "I'm forbidden by the new school president from allowing the phrase *white privilege* to be used in our chapel services."

His words saddened me. How can we exclude certain words from our discussions before even hearing the context in which they are used? Christians can sometimes be the worst offenders in this regard when we feel defensive.

My second emotion was probably more appropriate. I thought, *How must it feel for my Christian brothers and sisters of color when overt and subtle forms of racism still persist, yet Christian institutions censor phrases that would help us to be honest about our history and theology of race?*

Avoiding conversations or denying history is usually a charge we Americans level against other countries. Freedom of speech is what we treasure. Or so we think.

Our desire for comfort leads us to defensiveness when we are confronted with questions of race. But when did our comfort become the driving value?

Many people still use the word *colorblind*. It used to be a common phrase for talking about a post-racial way of living. The truth is, however, that not seeing skin color is a form of not seeing reality. Reality not seen is reality that cannot be affirmed. "Colorblindness" is a way we remain blind to the many subtle ways we're still dealing with a white standard. Colorblindness can lead to a comfort in not seeing or not calling out the need for diversity where it belongs.

I went on a tour of historically black colleges with friends on a trip designed to encourage the next generation of leaders of color. Before I left, I told someone about the trip, and the response was a snide comment: "'Black colleges'—that's so racist! Just imagine what they would say if we had 'white colleges.'" This kind of comment is all too common. On the surface it seems logical. Such a comment expects race to function like a math equation, with the dominant culture expecting an equal sign between two colors whenever it perceives a dissimilarity that makes it question fairness. We cannot look for similarity, however, without regard to history.

Racism isn't a math equation. It's a historical sin that remains a contemporary challenge. The historically black colleges were founded during a segregated time in America, when promising young black men and women weren't allowed to go to the elite colleges that white students attended. In fact, the four historically black colleges we visited in Atlanta (Clark Atlanta University, Spelman College, Morehouse College, and the Morehouse School of Medicine) share a single section of land in southwest Atlanta—their borders all touch one another. Like four people standing with their backs together for a degree of protection in a hostile environment, these schools banded together. Each school, existing in the Jim Crow South, experienced various forms of trial and terror both to property and to persons. Together, they were safer.

Today they remain the largest contiguous consortium of African American university students in the United States. So we don't simply say "black colleges," but rather Historically Black Colleges and Universities or HBCUs. Born in the midst of intense racism, they remain a strong part of African American history and culture and have a legacy of producing some of our nation's top entertainers and intellectuals. To say, "Why are there all-black colleges but not all-white colleges?" is to completely miss the fact that for much of America's history, all colleges were almost entirely white.

Historically black colleges were black by necessity, not choice, and they remain strong historical symbols of the priority of education and perseverance in the African American community.

UNDERSTANDING HOW PRIVILEGE WORKS

The creation of a white standard in the world during the age of exploration, and the white structural privilege prevalent for so long in America, led to what is often called "white privilege."

This is hard for many people to fully understand and believe. Some point out that a steep decline in life expectancy is happening right now among poor *white* men due to suicide, liver failure from alcoholism, overdose from opiates, and more. Many white people are struggling financially and simply don't feel like they're experiencing any privilege. Earning power has stagnated, and the cost of living is increasing. Many people, regardless of race or education, are feeling hopeless.

Is talking about white privilege just a way of making white people feel guilty, responsible for what is happening to poor people of color, or does it imply that there is some expectation that white people are not living up to? How are we to understand white privilege?

I often find myself in conversation with a hardworking American, someone who has struggled to make ends meet, and having to insist that white privilege is real.

On one such encounter, I was talking with a young white man running a landscaping service that constructed backyard landscapes, ponds, and fountains. He was very proud of his work ethic and told me that nobody had ever given him anything in life. In short, he believed he hadn't benefited from any privilege.

I asked him in what part of town he did most of his work.

"In the suburbs," he said.

I then asked where, specifically, he did his work.

"Mostly in people's backyards," he answered.

I asked him when he did most of his work.

"Well, during the day, of course," he quickly retorted.

I asked if I could pose one more question, and he said yes. So I asked him how he got most of his business.

He responded, "I put flyers in people's doors and sometimes knock at houses where I think there's a particular opportunity I can offer them."

Having gathered all this information about his business and how his work functions, I asked, "If you were a young man of color in those mostly white suburbs, is it possible you would be received differently by some of the potential clients?

"For instance, if you were a young black man proposing to work in the backyards of those suburbanites during the day when they're not home, is it possible some of your clients might show a degree of suspicion or bias? If you were Hispanic, talked with an accent, or looked like you were from a culture unfamiliar to the suburban communities where people can afford backyard ponds and fountains, do you think it might—even if ever so slightly—affect how successful you are when you knock on doors to talk to people about possible yard projects?"

He nodded, and I could see from the look on his face that he finally understood white privilege. White privilege doesn't mean your life isn't hard. It means that if you are a person of color, simply by virtue of that, your life might be harder.

Richard Rohr, Franciscan friar and international speaker, wrote one of the best descriptions of white privilege:

> White privilege is largely hidden from our eyes if we are white. Why? Because it is structural instead of psychological, and we tend to interpret most things in personal, individual, and psychological ways. Since we do not consciously have racist attitudes or overt racist behavior, we kindly judge ourselves to be open minded, egalitarian, "liberal," and therefore surely not racist. Because we have never been on the other side, we largely do not recognize the structural access, the trust we think we deserve, the assumption that we always belong and do not have to earn our belonging, the "we set the tone" mood that we white folks often live inside of—and take totally for granted and even naturally deserved. Only the outsider can spot all these attitudes in us. It is especially hidden in countries and all groupings where white people are the majority.[20]

When we look at a river, it's easy to see that the middle, where the current flows, is much different from the edges, where little pools are formed and things can stagnate. White privilege has meant, historically, that you've been born into the middle of the river, where things flow more easily.

White privilege means that even if you're the unluckiest white person born in the United States, you were still born into a fortunate race. It may not always be like this, and things might be changing fast (this is what many debates during the 2016 election cycle centered on), but the privilege afforded to the white race in modern Western history is undeniable.

Like Dinesh D'Souza, there is nowhere I'd rather live. But even if we have turned off the spigot of state-sponsored racism (which arguably we haven't), it doesn't mean the water has fully run out of the hose. We don't enter a post-racial era simply by wanting to; that will require knowing and being honest about our history—and being willing to work toward equality and end discrimination. Eliminating the traces of racism that remain within society and ourselves requires that we understand where that racism came from.

TWO

WHEN THE WORLD BECAME RACIST

Color in the Western Tradition

We admit that the same nature exists in
every race, and the same virtue.

CLEMENT OF ALEXANDRIA (CA. 150–215)

The myth of race is, at its heart, about power relations, and
in order to understand how it evolved, we must avoid vague
theoretical and ahistorical formulations and instead ask,
Who benefited from these narratives of racial difference,
and how, where, and under what conditions? Race signifies
neither a biological fact nor a primal prejudice, and it
lacks coherence of robust political ideology; rather, it is a
collection of fluid, contingent mythologies born of (among
other imperatives) fighting a war, assembling a labor force,
advancing the designs of demagogues, organizing a labor
union, and preserving voting and public schooling as privileges
reserved for some, rather than as rights shared by all.

JACQUELINE JONES, *A DREADFUL DECEIT*

WHEN WE ADDRESS RACISM, we often make the mistake of
trying to resolve the problem without diagnosing or understanding
what or who created it in the first place. What *is* racism? When did

racism begin? How, why, and among whom? Who benefited from racism? Under what conditions and under whose authority did it occur? How was it able to permeate societies and take firm root in cultures across history?

Most of us have probably never thought about it. If we have, we assume that racism is nearly as old as humanity itself and that it is an ever-present aspect of Western civilization. But that is not true.

Racism is a relatively new thing.

Again, most of us would likely assume that racism is merely a human tendency, something that—rightly or wrongly—comes naturally to us. But this, too, is not true.

Racism was appropriated as a handy way of justifying—in the name of conquest and even of religion—the robbery, subjugation, enslavement, and murder of entire people groups.

The idea behind racism—that one can differentiate between people based on their "race" and then assign different values to them on the basis of that judgment—was deliberately fostered with self-serving goals in mind. And the hugely successful instigation of this program of racism occurred just a few centuries ago.

You may be skeptical of the claims I just made. I recognize the need to support them, and I'll do that. But first let's look at the issue from a scientific angle.

SCIENCE AND RACE

As an aside—albeit an important one—the concept of humanity's being divisible into different races has no scientific validity. This has always been the case, even before the advent of rapid global travel enabled the further mixing of people from different parts of the world. The characteristics we focus on when categorizing others as different from us—skin color, facial features, hair texture—are found on a continuum of variation that confounds distinction. It is *discontinuity* that allows taxonomists and conservation biologists to differentiate between two races within a species of bird or within a species of frog, and that sort of discontinuity simply doesn't exist within human beings. Winfried Corduan states the consensus among anthropologists: "Human physical characteristics, including coloration, if graphed on a map of the world, show smooth transitions on both the north-south and east-west axes."[1]

To take this tangent a bit further, these features that so impress us when we look at one another are extremely superficial. Beneath the skin we are all basically the same—and this is especially true at the genetic level. Genetically speaking, I (with my rather unmixed Dutch heritage) am more similar to a male Maori than I am to any female, including my own mother and daughters. Whatever genetic differences the Maori man and I might have throughout the rest of our twenty-three pairs of chromosomes, they are fewer than the number of gene differences between men (with one X- and one Y-chromosome) and women (who have two X-chromosomes), even when a man and woman are closely related.

Indeed, the most remarkable thing about the genetics of humanity is how *little* diversity it contains in comparison to other populations of creatures, including other primates. The entire human population displays far less genetic diversity than that of chimpanzees, bonobos, or orangutans.[2] This is especially surprising given how much more widely human beings are spread across the globe, and how numerous we are, compared to any of these other species.

What's more, a significantly greater portion of humans' meager genetic differences involves *within*-population, rather than *between*-population, variability.[3] That is, the number of genetic differences among all Norwegians—or among all Nigerians—is greater than the number of genetic differences that could be used to distinguish between Norwegians and Nigerians. Externally, a Norwegian and a Nigerian look very different; but their respective genomes are quite similar, even within the genes that code for melanin and thereby determine skin color. Such genes differ only by a very few nucleotides, and the adaptive change that led to light skin occurred more than once as humans migrated to northerly latitudes.[4]

Distinguishing among people groups on the basis of race is an artificial, superficial venture with no scientific credibility. Of course, this reality is less important than the perception. Even though race has no anthropological or genetic grounding, our modern world is preoccupied with identifying differences between people groups and basing our behaviors on those perceived differences.

For much of modern history, we have associated "slavery" with black bodies. Even though there were Native American and white slaves throughout our nation's history, our idea of slavery was deeply shaped by America's entanglement with and dependence on the African slave trade. Given the mental picture of a slave, it's surprising to most people to learn that the etymology of the word *slave* derives from "slav," referring to the white Slavic people of central and Eastern Europe who were often at war with the Ottomans and thus frequently traded in the Ottoman slave markets.

As with racism itself, the concept of slavery was deeply affected by the age of exploration and subsequent colonial exploitation of new or discovered lands.

One of the ways we can locate the emergence of racial thinking based on color is by looking at literature and the history of ideas. Philosophers over the past several hundred years have said some of the most striking words on race, but first let's look at William Shakespeare, who lived in the 1500s. Shakespeare did much to influence the English language and, through his plays, reflected the ideas and culture of his day.

RACE AND SHAKESPEAREAN ENGLAND

William Shakespeare is widely regarded as the greatest English writer; his many plays are an enduring legacy of Elizabethan English customs and thought. And because the characters in his dramas were not all white Europeans but included dark-skinned foreigners—some, such as Othello, in central roles—the question of Shakespeare's view of race has become its own subdivision of Shakespearean scholarship.[5] From our modern vantage point, scholars are interested in whether Shakespeare himself can be considered to have been racist and, more broadly, what the English of his day thought about issues of race.

My reading of such scholarship leads me to several inferences. The first is how difficult it is for us to objectively assess the attitudes of people living several centuries ago. It is all too easy to attribute our own assumptions about race to Shakespeare and his sixteenth-century contemporaries rather than to set those assumptions aside and read such old texts for their own meaning.

I also find there is a real scarcity of unambiguous material (despite the breadth of the Shakespearean corpus) for drawing any conclusion about English views about race. For the most part, Shakespeare's characters of color are just that—they help to round out his cast by inclusion of some of the variety of humanity that existed in the England of his day, but they do so largely without explicit value judgment, political utility, or the sort of generalizing about a people group with which we are familiar today.

Finally, in those few cases in which Shakespeare seems to make a characterization or judgment of a foreign group, it is the religious difference that is more fundamentally in view than are differences in skin color. The Jews in *The Merchant of Venice*, for example, are notable more for their being non-Christian than for their being Semitic. And Othello's skin color matters less than his role as a military hero and an opponent of the "infidel" Turks.

In short, it seems that the England of Shakespeare's day was only beginning to be aware of foreigners who looked and thought differently. That is, the whole idea of classifying people according to their skin color was a relatively new thing, and Elizabethan England was still coming to grips with this notion. Racism had not yet evolved to the point where most English—or most Europeans—viewed other people as fundamentally different based on their ethnicity.

At that time, travel to Africa, the Americas, and India had only very recently begun to make Europeans aware that among humanity there was a much greater diversity of appearances than those with which they had long been familiar. G. K. Hunter argues that for the culture in which Shakespeare lived, it was much easier to characterize and caricature the *familiar* (European) "other," and to do so based on na-tional—not racial—distinctions, than to do so with the less familiar dark-skinned foreigner.[6] Shakespeare and his audience knew how to stereotype Italians, Dutch, Germans, and Irish, but their awareness of foreigners across the seas was as yet too shallow to provide much fodder for caricaturing.

A SURVEY OF PHILOSOPHY

Another way of establishing the timing of the advent of racism is to look back to an earlier period and examine the works of the great philosophers of history. Aristotle was exclusivist regarding who was qualified to be a full citizen and participate in the discourse regarding government. His criteria for inclusion did not involve race or ethnicity, however, but wealth and leisure time, which allowed an individual to develop his contemplative faculties. (Yes, Aristotle did show a gender bias here.) Aristotle believed that some people were fit only to be slaves, but among these he included some of his own countrymen. There is no sign of racism in Aristotle's writings.

And the same is likewise true of the medieval philosophers Mai-monides, Avicenna (Ibn Sīnā), and Thomas Aquinas, each of whom sought to synthesize Aristotelian philosophy with the beliefs of his own religion (Judaism, Islam, and Christianity, respectively). Going beyond Aristotle, Maimonides and Avicenna saw whole people groups as fit only for slavery, but the criterion that distinguished these groups was more clearly their lack or denial of the proper religion rather than their skin color or ethnicity.

Among notable philosophers, it is not until the seventeenth century that actual racism can be found, and even here it is not universal. For the "rationalist" philosophers such as René Descartes and G. W. Leibniz, the thing that distinguished all human beings was reason, and this characteristic was universal among humanity. (This seems to me a product—or at least a shadow—of the Christian doctrine of *imago Dei*.)

> The three main philosophers usually classed as "empiricists" [John Locke, George Berkeley, and David Hume] have much more to answer for with regard to race than the three "rationalists." Locke participated in the slave trade in various ways, Berkeley owned slaves, and Hume produced one of the first clear statements of a racist (or racialist) doctrine. By contrast, Descartes, [Baruch] Spinoza, and Leibniz did not clearly state racialist or racist sentiments, nor [are they known] to have engaged in activities that were associated with such sentiments.[7]

Although there is some overlap among the lives of the philosophers of these two schools (Locke was a contemporary of Leibniz and Spinoza), what we see is a development toward increasing racism beginning in the seventeenth century. Hume—the latest of those mentioned so far—wrote, "I am apt to suspect the negroes, and in general all other species of men (for there are four or five different kinds) to be naturally inferior to the whites."[8]

Racism among philosophers becomes most obvious with German philosopher Immanuel Kant (1724–1804). Among his many recorded beliefs on race, a few will suffice. "Humanity exists in its greatest perfection in the white race. The yellow Indians have a smaller amount of talent. The Negroes are lower and the lowest are a part of the American peoples."[9] "So fundamental is the difference between the two races of man, and it appears to be as great in regard to mental capacities as in color."[10] Moreover, Kant believed that "all races will be extinguished . . . only not that of the whites."[11] The subsequent influence of Kant's racist views—particularly in Germany—cannot be overstated.

If racism grew into our collective consciousness, what explains its rise?

EXPLORATION, COLONIZATION, AND THE ORIGIN OF RACISM

Colonialism is a familiar word and concept. It's part of the history of Western civilization. In fact, it's part of the history of the world: in 1914, the high-water mark of colonialism and empire during World War I, 84 percent of the world was either a colonial power, a colony, or a former colony.[12] That's an astounding figure.

If you want to understand the world in which we live, and especially the racial scars and divides that still plague our world, you'll need to wrestle with colonialism. It is during the age of exploration and colonization—beginning in the 1400s—that we find the seeds of racism as we know it today.

Popular historian Thomas Cahill, well known for his breakout book *How the Irish Saved Civilization*, argues that the great population decline associated with the spread of the Black Death through Europe opened up a novel space for mobility among people who had previously been landless and unable to improve their lot, given the class distinctions that held sway until that time. This new mobility depended on the ability to exploit others (dead or alive) by taking what was once theirs. Writes Cahill,

> If I intend to make myself an exploiter of one kind or another
> . . . I must find something or someone *appropriate* to exploit,
> that is, something or someone virtually begging to be ripped off.
> And at this point we hear, almost for the first time in Western
> history, the sounds of [modern] racism. The ancient Greeks had

been racist, believing themselves to be *hoi aristoi*, the best, and all others to be seriously deficient, barbarians of one sort or another. But the Greek attitude never found a foothold in Catholic Europe; and the Christian Middle Ages, intolerant about religion, were full of cultural, rather than racial, chauvinism. Those who persecuted Jews and, more occasionally, Muslims within their midst were not racists, for they found their old antagonists quite acceptable the moment they converted to Christianity. Medieval people may have been anti-Judaic; they were not anti-Semitic.

But it is in this period that the African slave trade begins to get under way and the several varieties of humans—Canary Islanders, black Africans, the Irish tribes "beyond the Pale" of English colonization, and the native tribes of the Americas—begin to be dehumanized, casually considered subhuman, fit only for manual labor or worse. It is also in this period that we first hear mention of Jewish "blood"—at least in Spain, which serves as a harbinger of attitudes that will eventually infect all of Europe. And it is in the Spain of this period that the phrase *sangre azul* (blue blood) begins to be bandied about—in reference to those whose lightness of skin allows the blueness of their veins (particularly on the backs of their hands or the undersides of their arms) to be displayed for all to acknowledge.[13]

Note that when Cahill discusses Greek "racism" earlier in the above quote he is using the word in a loose sense to refer to looking down on outsiders or lower classes, but not in the modern sense of an exclusive prejudice based on color, which he is arguing for throughout the excerpt.

The etymology of the word *race*, as used with regard to people, can be traced only to the sixteenth century. Around 1500 the English word *race* carried the sense of a group with a common occupation; by the 1540s the word had evolved to refer to a generation of people; and it wasn't until about 1560 that it was used to denote a tribe, nation, or people of common ancestry. Race's "modern meaning of 'one of the great divisions of mankind based on physical peculiarities' is from 1774."[14]

The modern emergence of racism and preoccupation with racial identities can thus be located sometime after the Middle Ages, developing through the age of exploration and becoming fully established in the colonial era.

THE DOCTRINE OF DISCOVERY

Colonialism took exploitation to the level of nations and continents, and those exploited were entire ethnicities. The instigators and perpetrators included greedy European monarchs hungry for wealth, power, and glory, and the explorers, military commanders, and soldiers they financed or hired. But they also included popes, church authorities, religious orders, and zealous leaders motivated either by their own hunger for wealth, power, and glory or by a more spiritual thirst for church expansion and conversion in an age dominated by the religious competition between Catholics and Protestants.

In order to justify colonialism, an idea like white supremacy was needed. The concept that whites were chosen by God and superior to people of color, who were less intelligent, less deserving, and savage, was born out of this need. White supremacy provided the political, social, and religious permission to claim lands not previously governed by "Christian" white people and to conquer, exterminate, and subjugate the allegedly inferior races found there. The African slave trade and the brutality toward, indeed genocide of, the people inhabiting the Americas (and elsewhere) were licensed by an unholy union of nationalist and religious zeal.

Despite being embraced by the religious leaders of the day, colonialism and the new racism that justified it were, of course, anything but Christian.

By now most of us recognize that the famous words from the US Declaration of Independence—"we hold these truths to be self-evident, that all men are created equal"—did not apply to "all human beings, regardless of gender, ethnicity, and such" in the minds of its author and signers. We may acknowledge that there is an ongoing, and unfinished, struggle to achieve equality for all individuals and groups who make up this nation. But most of us are not aware of how deeply ingrained in the minds of the nation's founders was the idea that uncivilized, unchristian people of color are less than human and therefore have no rights. In fact, these ideas are deeply embedded in our founding documents. For the purposes of this chapter, it is worthwhile to share a few more historical evidences associated with this doctrine of discovery.

After the success of Christopher Columbus's first voyage, a controversy arose over whether the newly discovered lands belonged to Spain or to Portugal. The claims of the Spanish monarchs were strengthened by a series of bulls (official papal declarations) written in 1493 by Pope Alexander VI (known as the "Borgia Pope"), who was born in Spain. The third of these papal bulls, written on May 4, declared that any land not inhabited by Christians was (by the will of Almighty God) available to be "discovered," claimed, and used by Christians so that "the Catholic faith and the Christian religion [might] be exalted and be everywhere increased and spread, that the health of the souls be cared for and that barbarous nations be overthrown and brought to the faith itself."[15]

The resolution to the conflict between Spain and Portugal was not only a physical boundary line both countries could adhere to, but also the catalyst behind church doctrines that shaped the New World and governed the age of discovery, referred to today as the "doctrines of discovery."

Thus the "discovery" and exploitation of the Americas was—however motivated by greed and thirst for power—baptized by patriotic and religious justification and blessed by popes and other church leaders. The clearly racist "doctrine of discovery" undergirded the conquest, rape, enslavement, and genocide of nonwhites throughout the world, and particularly in Africa and the Americas.

Thomas Cahill describes how this played out, using the familiar example of Christopher Columbus. The very first thing Columbus described about the new land was the nakedness of its people, and this was done intentionally. According to Cahill, "the nakedness of the people puts them in a category"—the idea that these people were savages. He goes on to quote historian Felipe Fernández-Armesto:

> A late fifteenth-century reader would have understood that Columbus was confronting "natural men," not the citizens of a civil society possessed of legitimate political institutions of their own. The registering of this perception thus prepared the way for the next step, the ritual appropriation of sovereignty to the Castilian monarchs, with a royal banner streaming and a scribe to record the act of possession.[16]

Cahill also writes that commanders of subsequent expeditions developed "a little ritual for assuaging whatever dim objections their strangled consciences might have voiced about these adventures in exploitation." The European explorers would read a standard text aloud to the curious natives who came out to see the arriving visitors. Of course, the natives couldn't have understood what was being read. Cahill provides an example of one such text:

> Of all these nations God our Lord gave charge to one man, called Saint Peter, that he should be lord and superior of all the men in the world, that all should obey him . . . and he gave him the world for his kingdom and jurisdiction.
>
> Wherefore, as best we can, we ask and require that you consider what we have said to you . . . that you acknowledge the Church as the Ruler and Superior of the whole world.

But if you do not do this, and maliciously make delay in it, I certify to you, that with the help of God, we shall powerfully enter into your country, and shall make war against you in all ways and manners that we can, and shall subject you to the yoke and obedience of the Church and of their Highness; we shall take you, and your wives, and your children, and shall make slaves of them, and as such shall sell and dispose of them as their Highnesses may command; and we shall take away your goods, and shall do you all the mischief and damage that we can, as to vassals who do not obey, and refuse to receive their lord, and resist and contradict him: and we protest that the deaths and losses which shall accrue from this are your fault, and not that of their Highnesses, nor ours, nor of these cavaliers who accompany us.[17]

Did you catch that?

If native peoples, in their own lands, did not recognize the authority of the church (an impossible thing even to understand, much less to submit to), the explorers would powerfully enter the country to subjugate them and make slaves of them all. Further, any loss of life and property would be the fault of the *victims themselves* for not becoming Christians immediately.

Can you dream of a more ghastly or horribly ironic way for Christians to greet strangers in the name of Christ?

This is, perhaps, not the place to rehearse all of the injustices—the enslavement, rape, robbery, extermination—that have resulted from this racist project from the age of exploration and colonialism, and there are many sources for learning about that age and its horrors.[18] Suffice it to say that there is a great deal for Americans of European descent and for Christians today to lament, repent of, and do our best to address and redress. The point for now, though, is simply to establish that the roots of the racism that continues to plague our culture today are to be found in the deliberate programs of "Christian" Europeans near the end of the fifteenth century.

POSTCONQUEST RACISM AGAINST NATIVE AMERICANS

But it would be wrong to move on without making clear that these racial ideas that allowed for colonialism remained entrenched long after the Native Americans were conquered, subjugated, confined to reservations, and, in many cases, driven to extinction. Indeed, these ideas remain alive today and have never been abolished, recanted, or rejected by our legal systems and documents.[19]

The doctrine of discovery and its underlying racism live on in the United States judicial system. In the 1823 Supreme Court case *Johnson v. McIntosh*, a case regarding the legal rights of Native Americans, the decision was based on the upholding of this racist doctrine. In a unanimous decision against the Native plaintiff, Chief Justice John Marshall's opinion held "that the principle of discovery gave European nations an absolute right to New World lands."[20] American Indians had only a right of occupancy, which was a lesser claim than the right of ownership imputed to Europeans by the doctrine of discovery.

My late friend and Christian brother Richard Twiss wrote a powerful book that lays out many of the horrors perpetrated on Native Americans quite recently. Many of these atrocities were committed by well-meaning government employees, social workers, and Christian missionaries. Because Twiss's message is primarily to today's church and focuses on hope for the future, he doesn't spend much time describing these disastrous programs. But they include the reservation system, the Relocation Act, and the horror of a compulsory boarding-school program. Regarding the latter, Twiss relates the story of Lynda, who was five years old when she was torn from her family, home, and tribe and forcibly taken, with her siblings, to a boarding school in 1960.

When they arrived, Lynda and her brothers were separated; she would not see them again for a long time. She and the other girls were taken to a dormitory, where they all had their clothes removed and were showered. Each girl's hair was cut in exactly the same way, and they were given dress uniforms to wear. The girls were told they would not be called by their names anymore; instead they were given numbers. For the rest of the year Lynda was called "63."

Lynda remembers that one morning when they were in the showers, one of the other girls was singing a hymn in her native language. A nun came and dragged her out of the shower and began strapping her for speaking in her language. The little girl knew only a smattering of English and in her fitful state could plead only in her own language, asking why she was being punished. This provoked the nun to strap her even more. This incident planted in Lynda a seed of hatred toward White people and their religion. . . .

Lynda's story is not atypical among Native families. The residential schools that the children were carried off to created generations of emotionally scarred children, some of whom are still alive today, having grown to adulthood without the nurture and care of being raised by loving parents or other adult relatives. . . .

The heartache and suffering of this kind of child abuse do not disappear with time. If not healed, they only grow worse.[21]

Citing research by R. Pierce Beaver, Twiss characterizes Christian missions among the native peoples who resided in North America:

The historical record of missions among the tribes of North America is a saga marked by enormous potential, great failures and profound sadness. With a few notable exceptions—men like Sir William Johnson, Chief Joseph Brant and Rev. Charles Chauncy—those engaged in eighteenth-century mission work disdained Native American culture and barred it from the churches. Early missionaries failed to recognize and embrace the intrinsic God-given value of the people to whom they were sent—a blindness that has prevailed in the American church to this day.[22]

Almost every aspect of the history of white men's interaction with Native Americans is contrary to God's commands. God condemns all who make themselves rich at the expense of others; he condemns robbery, rape, and murder. Moreover, it is God who created every human being in his image and decreed where they should live. Christ's death was to reconcile all people (indeed, all created things) to himself (Colossians 1:20).

I have to admit that it wasn't until several years ago, largely through the work of friends such as Richard Twiss and Mark Charles, that I realized the full extent of the sinister role the church played in the age of conquest. Mark Charles has been working tirelessly to shed light on the doctrine of discovery, but you and I may well wonder why we never learned how Western slavery and subjugation got its legitimizing religious push.

Learning about this part of history has opened my eyes to myriad hostile stereotypes in movies and TV. It also brought great shock to me when, several years back at our church's summer camp, I found our summer interns rehearsing a skit in which Native Americans would burst in and kidnap frontier women. I quickly put an end to the skit but remain deeply troubled at how easily and unthinkingly we can fall into racial stereotyping based on the narratives we heard as we grew up in the dominant culture.

Colonialism split the world of humanity into different colors. It is high time that we set such division aside forever and return to seeing the world as it was seen before the age of exploration and colonialism.

THE BIBLE AND RACE

While throughout history many have used the Bible to find justification for slavery and prejudice, a truly biblical understanding of humanity recognizes that all human beings have equal worth, and the only reason for this worth is our creation in the image of God (Genesis 1:26-27). This fundamental doctrine has vast implications for morality and justice. The phrase *human race* is used six times in the Old Testament, each time referring to the whole species. When the Bible speaks of difference, it points to language, tribe, or nation; it does not categorize people on the basis of skin color.

Due to our sin nature, human beings are bound to fall far short of creating social systems and governments that recognize and fully honor the biblical doctrine of human equality. Instead, we discriminate and devalue people on the basis of gender, skin color, mental capacity, functional capability, age, citizenship, and other traits.

The New Testament reiterates the concept that all humanity is equal. A new commitment to abolish walls of division flows out of the incarnation, teachings, death, and resurrection of Jesus. Thus the apostle Peter can say, "I now realize how true it is that God does not show favoritism" (Acts 10:34). Paul writes the same to the church in Rome (Romans 2:11), and James warns against showing partiality (James 2:1, 9). For the early followers of Christ, this idea of the unity of all humanity was radically countercultural; nonetheless, Paul expresses it clearly in his letter to the Galatians: "There is neither Jew nor Gentile, neither slave nor free, nor is there male and female, for you are all one in Christ Jesus" (Galatians 3:28).

There can be no mistake: in creating this world, God ultimately intended that we all be valued equally. The church in the age of exploration missed this, and the American church in the age of Manifest Destiny missed it as well.

While slavery may be a more familiar category in our minds, the subjugation and exploitation of black Americans after emancipation is less familiar. This is one of the stories, perhaps, where we can best see how institutionalized racism morphed into countless forms of terror and exploitation—the consequences and vestiges of which still exist and perpetuate inequity today.

THREE

STOLEN LABOR

In order to get beyond racism, we must first take
account of race. There is no other way.

HARRY A. BLACKMUN (1908-1999)

The American church avoids lament. The power of lament
is minimized and the underlying narrative of suffering that
requires lament is lost. But absence doesn't make the heart
grow fonder. Absence makes the heart forget. The absence
of lament in the liturgy of the American church results in the
loss of memory. We forget the necessity of lamenting over
suffering and pain. We forget the reality of suffering and pain.

SOONG-CHAN RAH, *PROPHETIC LAMENT: A CALL FOR
JUSTICE IN TROUBLED TIMES*

PRESIDENT ABRAHAM LINCOLN was swept into his second
term as president in 1864 largely due to General Ulysses S. Grant's
victories in the summer of that year. Prior to that, Lincoln decided to
change the vice presidential candidate to Andrew Johnson, who ap-
pealed to pro-Union southerners. Lincoln knew he needed their
support in his efforts to rebuild the South once the Civil War ended as
well as to broaden his appeal when his reelection chances looked slim.

John Wilkes Booth's assassination of Lincoln, in one of the most
tragic twists of history ever, not only ended President Lincoln's life but
also put a southern Democrat into the Oval Office. Sympathetic with

Southerners, Johnson would later stall Reconstruction initiatives and take an apathetic stance toward the plight of the freed slaves, for which he was impeached and nearly removed from office by those seeking to fulfill Lincoln's legacy. Lincoln's assassination had a tremendous impact on inhibiting true freedom and equality for Americans of African descent living in the South.

RECONSTRUCTION

Reconstruction was a brief period of great black progress. Lasting from 1865 to 1877, it focused on the transformation and reincorporation of the South after the Civil War. During Reconstruction, African Americans were given the right to vote. This Fifteenth Amendment right was underscored by Enforcement Acts, which protected their right to vote, hold office, serve on juries, and receive equal protection under the law. Further, the Enforcement Acts gave the federal government the ability to intervene if a state was not effectively enforcing the law. During this time some beautiful and amazing minds also emerged. W. E. B. Du Bois said of this period, "The slave went free; stood a brief moment in the sun; then moved back again toward slavery."[1]

As Du Bois wrote, the progress was not to last. While there were a number of factors that led to short-lived reconstruction efforts, the result was continued black oppression.

When the Civil War ended, the South could not challenge the outlawing of slavery. However, although the institution was gone, the belief system remained intact. White southerners within the power structures looked for ways to replace the labor pool that was lost as well as to keep African Americans in a subservient place. They systematically curtailed black progress through disenfranchisement, intimidation, political policy, the criminal justice system, and legal manipulation. In a desperate, century-long effort to maintain their power, southern whites created a series of intricate systems of oppression.

The new racial caste system emerging after Reconstruction had a name: Jim Crow. Exactly where the term *Jim Crow* first came from is unclear. In 1832, Thomas D. Rice had written a minstrel song and dance called "Jump Jim Crow." Within several years the name had come to be used as a descriptor, with "Jim Crow law" first appearing in 1904.[2]

Discrimination and segregation were not just southern practices; they occurred in the North as well. But in the South, white supremacy and dominion over blacks was the number-one public concern and took on a strikingly different tone from in the North.[3] Eventually laws and customs of segregation extended to churches, schools, housing, jobs, eating and drinking, public transportation, recreation, medical care, orphan care, marriage, prisons, asylums, and on to funeral homes, morgues, and cemeteries.[4] No aspect of life was untouched by racial divides.

Segregation was primarily a matter of custom until the Supreme Court's decision in *Plessy v. Ferguson* in 1896. In that case, the court found that the Constitution did not require the elimination of racial distinction but only the equal treatment of races. That is, the Supreme Court decreed that the Fourteenth Amendment did not prohibit distinguishing between citizens on the basis of race.[5] And with this conclusion, "separate but equal" became the law for decades. This decision did not create or cause the spread of Jim Crow, which had begun long before the decision. However, it provided a legal basis for continuing to view people as "black Americans" or "white Americans," and not simply as "Americans." As Jerrod Packard writes, "The Plessy decision struck an almost fatal blow to what was left of nineteenth-century black aspirations for equality and for assimilation into America's vaunted melting pot."[6]

Decades later, the "separate but equal" concept would be used by Thurgood Marshall and his legal team to frame their argument against school segregation in the 1954 landmark case *Brown v. Board*

of Education of Topeka. Marshall and his team cited research conducted in the 1940s by psychologists Kenneth and Mamie Clark.
Their "doll test" involved showing white and black dolls to African
American children living in New York and Washington, DC. The
children's reactions to black dolls were demonstrably more negative
than their reactions to the white dolls.

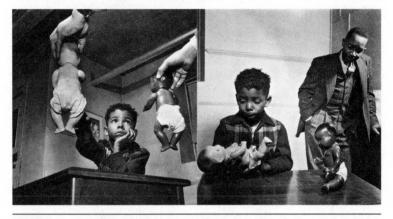

Figure 1. The Clark doll test. Photographs by Gordon Parks. Courtesy of and copyright The Gordon Parks Foundation.

Though by this time the civil rights movement had begun, it would
be many years before the psychological effects of segregation were
understood. One hundred years' worth of cultural and sociological
abuse wasn't going to be undone by simply abolishing the system that
had caused it.

SLAVERY BY ANOTHER NAME

Most of us are familiar with Jim Crow laws, but these laws were only
one small part of the problem. Sadly, segregation was only one of the
ways cultural racism had seeped into the legal system. Taking a deeper
look at history, we find that although slavery had been abolished
during the Civil War, it was far from dead. A new legal system of
slavery emerged after the war ended: convict leasing.

In 1865, before Reconstruction, Governor Benjamin Humphreys of Mississippi passed a series of laws known as the Black Codes. Jim Crow and convict leasing were rooted in such laws. There were many laws selectively targeted at blacks, but the vagrancy laws requiring all blacks to have jobs proved most pernicious. At a time when jobs were scarce any black person unable to prove employment, if stopped by law enforcement, was convicted.[7]

Of the nine southern states that soon adopted these codes, eight allowed these convicts to be hired out to plantations and private companies for forced labor.[8] Du Bois later trenchantly explained, "The Codes spoke for themselves. . . . No open-minded student can read them without being convinced they meant nothing more nor less than slavery in daily toil."[9]

The codes were repealed during Reconstruction, but Reconstruction soon crumbled as white supremacist groups wielded organized terror and the federal government refused to respond. Soon new laws were passed in southern states, notably reviving the system of convict leasing. It would last for over sixty years across the South, enslaving hundreds of thousands of African Americans and generating millions of dollars for state governments, white-owned corporations, and wealthy individuals.

For example, in 1876 in Mississippi, the new post-Reconstruction government quickly enacted a series of laws aimed at blacks, including the Leasing Act, under which prisoners were "allowed" to "work outside the penitentiary in building railroads, levees or in any private labor or employment."[10] A system of subleasing developed whereby the state would lease convicts to a middleman, who would then lease them out to business owners. This allowed for more flexible labor and even worse conditions, as convicts were now working to profit three separate parties, each wanting to spend as little as possible in order to make as much as possible.[11]

The majority of convicts had been arrested for minor infractions such as stealing chickens, vagrancy, or gambling. In an 1898 convict-board report from Alabama, the column for recording reasons that convicts were imprisoned mostly says "not given."[12]

Sentence lengths varied. In some cases, convicts were fined. Unable to pay the fines, they were leased for as few as twenty days to a private company. However, often additional time was added to their sentence to cover fees owed to law enforcement and others involved in their original prosecution.[13] In other cases, sentences of ten years or more were imposed.

Tragically, the system did not discriminate by age. In Mississippi alone, hundreds of children were leased, and by 1880, 25 percent of convicts leased out for forced labor were children. Records show that some were as young as six.[14] That's unbelievable! Their grandchildren are the generation that fought for civil rights in the 1950s, over half a century later.

Doctors called to care for convicts documented the practice in their reports. One such doctor asked whether "a sovereign state can afford to send her citizens, for slight offenses, to a prison where, in the nature of things, a large number are condemned to die."[15] Similarly, in 1912 Governor George Donaghey of Arkansas called leasing "legalized murder that sentenced thousands of faceless victims to a 'death by oppression' for often trivial acts. Under no other system," he believed, "did the punishment so poorly fit the crime."[16]

There were high mortality rates among black convicts, indicative of deplorable work and living conditions. You might think that because convict leasing wasn't actual slavery, conditions wouldn't be so brutal. But in fact the opposite is true: because the business owners did not actually own the convicts, as they had during slavery, they had no incentive to keep them healthy; they could simply lease another convict at a low cost when one died.

A 1918 report on convict deaths in Alabama included the following causes: "Killed by convict, Asphyxia from Explosion, Tuberculosis, Burned by Gas Explosion, Pneumonia, Shot by Foreman, Gangrenous Appendicitis, Paralysis."[17] The mortality rate for convicts in Mississippi ranged between 9 and 16 percent in the 1880s. In 1882 the mortality rate among blacks leased out for hard labor was 17 percent, while the mortality rate for white convicts was only 2 percent. Former Mississippi state attorney general Frank Johnson called it an "epidemic death rate without the epidemic."[18]

Mississippi abolished the system of convict leasing in 1890, but the system remained in full force across the rest of the South for decades. Even as convict leasing to outside organizations ended with Alabama in 1927, for-profit labor in prisons themselves and through informal networks continued into the civil rights era. Many state governments developed their own prison camps and farms, such as Mississippi's infamous Parchman Farm, which in 1901 became known as the Mississippi State Penitentiary.[19]

While black convicts were being reenslaved, the South's economy was booming. Leased convicts built railroads, mined coal, and worked in lumber camps, in turpentine factories, and on sugar plantations. For example, convicts built most of the thirty-five hundred miles of railroad track in North Carolina during the railroad boom of the 1870s and 1880s.[20] Alabama had the largest system of convict leasing, and Tennessee Coal, Iron & Railroad Company was the greatest user of forced labor.[21] The correlation between convict leasing and the economic rebirth of the South is so strong that American historian David Oshinsky says, "The South's economic development can be traced by the blood of its prisoners."[22]

In Matthew 25:41-43 Jesus says, "Depart from me, you who are cursed, into the eternal fire prepared for the devil and his angels. . . . I was sick and in prison and you did not look after me." I can only imagine what Jesus would have to say about convict leasing in the Bible Belt through the decades, its shocking mortality rates, and the millions of people who benefited from the economic development it enabled. Capturing Jesus' command, vision, and perspective is the first step in deconstructing it, diagnosing it, and hopefully preventing its repetition.

In *Slavery by Another Name*, Pulitzer Prize–winning author Douglas Blackmon follows the story of convict leasing and its legacy through the life and family of Green Cottingham, who was leased to the Tennessee Coal, Iron & Railroad Company. Blackmon traces the lingering financial impact on companies and families into the 2000s. Not surprisingly, he encounters many companies, such as US Steel, that are reluctant to acknowledge their historical involvement and the financial benefit they gained. Such gains served to give them a leg up on their competitors who did not lease convicts and had to pay prevailing wages. Additionally, these same companies continually fail to accept any accountability for their past leadership.[23]

Blackmon's research showed that his own ancestors lived alongside and indirectly benefited from the labor of Cottingham and his ancestors. The greater awareness of the interconnectedness of history and injustice led Blackmon to summarize, "I had no hand in the horrors perpetrated by . . . twentieth-century slave masters who terrorized American blacks for four generations. But it is nonetheless true that hundreds of millions of us spring from or benefit as a result of lines of descent that abided those crimes and benefited from them."[24]

It is crucial that we understand that this history shapes modern civil rights issues and racial disparities today. Blackmon argues that the situation of African Americans is often portrayed as static since emancipation and neglects the continuing cycles of defeat.

An understanding of the era of convict leasing explains the felt frustration of the beleaguered advance of African Americans between the Civil War and the civil rights movement.[25] Blackmon writes: "Certainly, the great record of forced labor across the South demands that any consideration of the progress of civil rights remedy in the United States must acknowledge that slavery, real slavery, didn't end until 1945—well into the childhoods of the black Americans who are only now reaching retirement age."[26]

He further argues that this understanding is critical to understanding the situation of race relations in America today: "Only by acknowledging the full extent of slavery's grip on U.S. society, its intimate connections to present-day wealth and power, the depth of its injury to millions of black Americans, the shocking nearness in time of its true end—can we reconcile the paradoxes of current American life."[27]

Although the convict leasing system ultimately ended, use of the criminal justice system as a means of population control for minorities never fully went away. Ironically, systemic racism twisted into new forms following the great civil rights gains in 1964 and 1965.

DISENFRANCHISEMENT

While convict leasing was outlawed by the 1930s, other Jim Crow laws remained in place—including those establishing disenfranchisement. After emancipation and following the Reconstruction acts of 1867, nearly half of southern voters were black. In some states they constituted a majority of the voting population. In 1880, two-thirds of black men voted in the presidential election, and the number of black legislators elected in 1872 would not be matched again until the 1990s.[28]

However, starting with Mississippi in 1898 and ending with Georgia in 1908, all formerly Confederate states restricted voting rights for African Americans. Of course, the Fifteenth Amendment made it illegal to withhold voting based on race or country of origin, so such discrimination required creativity and intimidation. Laws were enacted restricting the right to vote based on crimes thought "black" while "white" crimes were largely disregarded. Residency requirements and poll taxes were imposed, as were measures of "good character," all designed to thwart blacks from voting while incorporating enough loopholes so that poor whites could still vote.

Such was the effect that while there had been 30,334 black voters registered in Louisiana in 1896, by 1900 there were only 5,320 black voters, and by 1910 only 730 remained. Similarly, over the same period, in Alabama the number dropped from over 180,000 to only 3,000, and in states such as Virginia and North Carolina, black voter turnout dropped to zero.[29]

Jim Crow formally ended with the Civil Rights Act of 1964 and the Voting Rights Act of 1965. The system had begun to weaken under mounting pressure from several areas, including the Supreme Court's segregation rulings as well as the various civil rights campaigns with which we are familiar. Many blacks had migrated to the North and gained political power, and the National Association for the Advancement of Colored People (NAACP), dating back to 1902, had been generating a stream of campaigns against Jim Crow laws in federal courts.

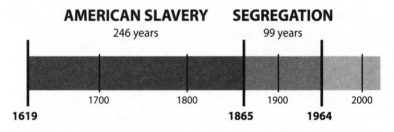

AMERICAN SLAVERY   SEGREGATION
246 years   99 years
1700   1800   1900   2000
1619   1865   1964

Figure 2. State-sponsored discrimination in America

The degree and duration of state-sponsored slavery and denial of civil rights in the United States are shocking when we consider how some of the periods of greatest injustice occurred contemporaneously with what are regarded as our greatest commitments to liberty—fighting World War II and opposing communism in the Cold War. This discrepancy presents an important warning when we consider justice issues today.

As Americans, when we criticize other countries and their policies, we often assume the morality or rightness of our own policies. But our country's oppression of African Americans certainly reveals our potential for blind spots. During the time of Jim Crow, leaders of other countries, including the Soviet Union after the Russian Revolution, consistently noted the treatment of blacks in America. It was a continual sticking point in the debates around the drafting of the Universal Declaration of Human Rights, led by Eleanor Roosevelt—a declaration that was drafted while Jim Crow and segregation still existed.[30]

One of the more interesting experiences I've had in considering the issue of race was watching the documentary *Freedom Riders* with my two older daughters. This documentary includes Soviet news footage and coverage of the Mother's Day bus bombing by racists in Alabama during the Freedom Ride of 1961. The attack was made famous by the brazen terrorism and by the iconic picture of black smoke billowing out of the sides of a Greyhound bus, with black and white Freedom Riders coughing and in turmoil on the grass in the foreground. Seeing history reported accurately from the viewpoint of the Soviet Union was a weird experience for me. I grew up during the Cold War, and I always assumed the United States was superior and more truthful than its Cold War adversaries. Turns out that history is far more complex than how it was portrayed by Hollywood in the movies I watched as a teen.

NIXON'S SOUTHERN STRATEGY

Though one caste system ended in 1965, another was born just six years later. In June 1971, President Nixon declared a "war on drugs." Publicly, it addressed the increasing use of heroin, marijuana, and hallucinogens. But subsequent accounts confirm that the "war" was racially motivated. *Harper's Magazine* recently released a twenty-two-year-old interview conducted by Dan Baum with John Erlichman, Nixon's domestic policy chief and Watergate coconspirator. With shocking candor, Erlichman explained:

> We knew we couldn't make it illegal to be either against the war
> or black, but by getting the public to associate the hippies with
> marijuana and blacks with heroin and then criminalizing both

heavily, we could disrupt those communities. We could arrest their leaders, raid their homes, break up their meetings, and vilify them night after night on the evening news. Did we know we were lying about the drugs? Of course we did.[31]

Erlichman was no longer living at the time the interview was released, and thus he was unable to either confirm or deny these remarks. But his comment isn't the only evidence that Nixon's administration was deliberately targeting black communities. Nixon's 1968 campaign is a shocking case of deliberate, racially charged political machination.

In an effort to distance itself from the civil rights movement and the needs and plight of African Americans, Nixon bet (correctly) that if African Americans joined the Democratic Party, white southerners would turn Republican, tipping the scales in that party's favor. This Republican gambit has been dubbed the "Southern Strategy." In a 1970 interview, Nixon's political strategist Kevin Philips said:

> From now on, the Republicans are never going to get more than 10 to 20 percent of the Negro vote and they don't need any more than that . . . but Republicans would be shortsighted if they weakened enforcement of the Voting Rights Act. The more Negroes who register as Democrats in the South, the sooner the Negrophobe whites will quit the Democrats and become Republicans. That's where the votes are. Without that prodding from the blacks, the whites will backslide into their old comfortable arrangement with the local Democrats.[32]

In other words, Philips said that the Republican Party should abandon black voters. At the same time, they should allow the Voting Rights Act, which ensured voting rights for minorities, to be enforced, as it would flood the Democratic Party with black voters, thereby chasing all the white racist voters into the Republican Party. The Southern

Strategy was built around the behavior and voting patterns of reactionary and racist whites. And it worked.

Although Philips popularized the Southern Strategy, he did not create it,[33] and he was probably just doing his job. He later left the Republican Party and became one of its most outspoken critics.

The Southern Strategy and Philips's interview corroborate the sad truth that race played an important role in political strategy and campaigning, even if the public language was racially neutral. Even more fascinating than the corroborating strategies is what Erlichman said in another interview—one that is on record. He confirms, "There were subliminal racial messages in a lot of Nixon's campaigning." He goes on to say how he exploited Johnson's embrace of blacks and that Nixon saw blacks as "genetically inferior." Erlichman says of Nixon, "In his heart he was very skeptical about their ability to excel except in rare cases. He didn't feel this way about other groups. . . . He thought they couldn't achieve on a level with whites."[34]

Those at the center of political strategy are well aware that, for a long time, our political leaders have been complicit in reinforcing the racial stereotypes of parts of the electorate, practicing what is often referred to as race-baiting.

The role of race in political strategy is no small thing and has been documented and confirmed across myriad campaigns throughout US history. In a 1981 taped comment he thought was off the record, strategist Lee Atwater infamously described the abstraction of racial language and issues in campaigning when he said, "You start out in 1954 by saying, 'Nigger, nigger, nigger.' By 1968 you can't say 'nigger'—that hurts you, backfires. So you say stuff like, uh, forced busing, states' rights, and all that stuff, and you're getting so abstract. Now, you're talking about cutting taxes, and all these things you're talking about are totally economic things and a byproduct of them is, blacks get hurt worse than whites." He didn't confirm it as always explicitly intentional but claimed it at least reflected subconscious intent.[35]

The racialized politics of the war on drugs, a set of policies born in the 1960s, raged into the 1990s. It created a new racial caste system where people of color were stigmatized and held in an inferior position in society by custom and law—just like with slavery and Jim Crow.[36]

REAGAN'S WAR ON DRUGS

In a press conference in 1971, Nixon declared war on drugs by calling drug abuse America's "public enemy number one."[37] The "war" began primarily as an effort to treat addiction rather than fight crime. Jimmy Carter even attempted to introduce legislation decriminalizing the use of marijuana. But the the war on drugs didn't gain any significant traction until the second year of Ronald Reagan's first term.

In October 1982, President Reagan announced his administration's plan to cut funding for prevention and treatment of drug addiction and to increase funding to punish drug use. For example, FBI funding increased from $8 million in 1980 to $95 million in 1984, while the Department of Education's antidrug funds were cut from $14 million to $3 million.[38] This at a time when less than 2 percent of the population saw drugs as the most important issue facing America.[39]

At the same time the war on drugs was escalating, globalization and other changes in industry were under way, leaving fewer employment opportunities for those trapped in the inner cities—which increased the incentive to sell drugs.[40] Using sensational, radicalized imagery, the administration's media campaigns dramatized the emergence of crack cocaine while avoiding explicitly racist language. Though it was true that crack was damaging inner-city black neighborhoods, the United States chose to criminalize its use and exploit the justice system as a vehicle for racial control rather than focusing on prevention, as so many other industrialized countries do.[41]

Through all the campaigns, political initiatives, and media coverage, research showed that the level of public concern for drugs "was only weakly correlated with actual crime rates, but highly correlated with political initiatives, campaigns, and partisan appeals."[42]

The Anti–Drug Abuse Act of 1986 instituted mandatory minimum sentences for distribution of cocaine. The mandatory minimums were much harsher for crack—a drug associated primarily with black neighborhoods—than for powder cocaine, which was used primarily by wealthy whites.[43] In 1988 the punishments for drug offenses were increased and included civil penalties such as the elimination of access to public housing and other federal benefits such as student loans. The draconian laws continued to escalate from there. The sentencing disparity created by the 1986 legislation has since been corrected with the 2010 Fair Sentencing Act.

I was going through middle school and high school in the Greater Washington, DC, area in the 1980s and 1990s. I remember the heavy rhetoric about the war on drugs in the nightly newscasts as well as the terrifying perception that was generated regarding crack cocaine, which at the time was a significant problem in the nation's capital. My older sister Laura was finishing up her degree at George Mason Law School. She published her law review on the inequity in drug sentencing in the early 1990s, in an article that has since been cited in several Supreme Court decisions. It took me much longer to fully understand the consequences of the inequities that she grasped then.

Regarding these policies created under Reagan's war on drugs and Bill Clinton's tough-on-crime legislation, renowned African American author Michelle Alexander writes, "Ninety percent of those admitted to prison for drug offenses in many states were black or Latino, yet the mass incarceration of communities of color was explained in race-neutral terms—an adaptation to the needs and demands of the current political climate. The New Jim Crow was born."[44]

THE IMPLICATIONS

The pushback from many of the people I talk to likely would be along these lines: "If they did the crime, they need to do the time." This would seem like a simple and logical response, if not for several important factors—racial profiling in the drug war, inequitable legal sentencing, and abuses in the legal system—all of which create drastic racial disparities. Data show that whites and blacks use drugs at similar rates, and more whites are dealers; yet while African Americans make up roughly 13 percent of the US population, they make up 31 percent of all those arrested for drug violations and nearly 40 percent of those incarcerated for drug-related convictions.[45]

As noted, until recently, mandatory minimum sentences were exorbitantly higher for crack than for powder cocaine, a distinction arguably based on race. Although the two drugs share the same constituents, crack cocaine is cheaper and more prevalent in inner cities. The disparity in sentences points to a significant racial bias. Research also shows that prosecutors are twice as likely to seek a mandatory minimum sentence for African Americans as they are for whites facing the same charges.[46]

There are also great financial incentives for law enforcement to participate in the drug war, including incentives for the number of arrests and the legal authority to keep the majority of cash and other assets seized during a search for drugs.[47] To maximize points earned for felonies, police perform raids in neighborhoods where people are less likely to protest. Imagine frequent military-style police raids in a white suburban neighborhood.

Michelle Alexander summarizes it this way:

> Homes may be searched for drugs based on a tip from an unreliable, confidential informant who is trading the information for money or to escape prison time. And once swept into the system, people are often denied . . . meaningful representation

and pressured into plea bargains by the threat of unbelievably harsh sentences—sentences for minor drug crimes that are higher than many countries impose on convicted murderers.[48]

Eighty percent of criminal defendants in the drug war are unable to afford a lawyer, yet because of inadequacies in our legal system, many of them go without a public defender. A number of states deny a public defender to such defendants, no matter how impoverished, based on the belief that they should be able to afford their own. For example, in Wisconsin anyone who earns more than three thousand dollars *per year* is considered able to pay for their own lawyer.[49] Because of harsh sentencing and lack of legal support, many defendants choose to plead guilty to a lesser offense—even though they are not guilty at all. As the American Bar Association has reported, "All too often, defendants plead guilty, even if they are innocent, without really understanding their legal rights or what is occurring. . . . The fundamental right to a lawyer that Americans assume applies to everyone accused of criminal conduct effectively does not exist in practice for countless people across the United States."[50]

The implications of the drug war extend far beyond prison in the life of a convicted felon. Once a person is convicted of a felony, forms of diminishment and exclusion are legal. Convicted felons are often not allowed to vote or sit on juries; they cannot receive any public assistance; and it is legal to discriminate against them when they seek housing or a job. While in prison, prisoners accumulate fees so that when they are released, even if they are able to find a job in their neighborhood—which in some states can be incredibly difficult because of stipulations on getting a driver's license—their paycheck can be garnished to pay the escalating fees. This creates a cycle of stigma and isolation, and many give in and embrace their stigmatized identity.[51]

It's not hard to see how this is a caste system like slavery, Jim Crow, or convict leasing, even if on the surface it is colorblind. Because of its supposed colorblind nature, it goes unnoticed by most of us; somehow it is easier to believe that "the majority of young African American men in urban areas freely chose a life of crime than to accept the real possibility that their lives were structured in a way that virtually guaranteed their early admission into a system from which they can never fully escape."[52]

If law and justice are being applied fairly, then imprisonment rates of whites and blacks should be the same, in line with population proportions. Instead, more African American adults are under correctional control today than were enslaved in 1850, ten years before the Civil War began, and more are unable to vote than in 1870, the year the Fifteenth Amendment was passed.[53] Black men are imprisoned at six times the rate of white men; estimates indicate that black men have a one in three chance of going to prison in their lifetime.[54]

Although these policies have come under increasing scrutiny, some changes are being made, and the prison population is now slightly declining from its peak in 2009,[55] there is a long way to go. This modern history shows the hierarchy of value we've possessed and imposed on others well past the time of slavery, and it is continuing to the present day. We've simply gotten better at covering up or becoming blind to the racial nature of it—though the racial construct still exists both explicitly and implicitly in our lives and in the systems of our society.

I live in the state of Oregon, where marijuana is now legal, and other states have likewise legalized the sale of certain drugs. I find it ironic that white corporate businessmen now stand to make millions of dollars by selling a product that millions of young men, predominantly of color, are currently incarcerated for possessing in minuscule amounts.

I also find myself wondering what strong words Jesus would have for the history of our criminal justice system. If he uses words like *cursed* and *eternal fire* simply for the failure to care for prisoners, how much more contempt does he have for our system of justice and incarceration, which has exploited generations of people of color for profit and economic development? As my friend Soong-Chan implies in the epigraph that opened this chapter, the only appropriate response to the last two centuries of criminal justice in the United States is profound lament.

The dominant culture in America has rarely prioritized the pursuit of civil rights for minorities—it has often been a long, slow march. A thin personal gospel, along with an oversimplified understanding of deeply entrenched racial systems (what I've called "the myth of equality" in the title of this book), has often allowed race to be made secondary to other foreign, domestic, and spiritual concerns.

An honest assessment of history and its lingering effects, however, can show us how ongoing struggles with race and inequality result directly from our unwillingness to understand the plight of others, sacrifice for true equality of opportunity, and deal directly with racism. Let's look at a devastating instance of inequality of opportunity then and now: the shaping of neighborhoods and maps in the United States beginning in the mid-1900s.

FOUR

HOW OUR CITIES GOT THEIR SHAPE

The Great Migration, Redlining, and the Roots of Modern Segregation

In the wake of slavery and the Civil War, there was so much
ugliness in black life that one would have had to be blind not to
see it. And nothing, absolutely nothing, was uglier than lynching
in all of its many forms: hanging, burning, beating, dragging,
and shooting—as well as torture, mutilation, and especially
castration. And yet so many were blind, deaf, and dumb. What
enabled artists to see what Christian theologians and ministers
would not? What prevented these theologians and ministers,
who should have been the first to see God's revelation in black
suffering, from recognizing the obvious gospel truth? Did it
require such a leap of imagination to recognize the visual and
symbolic overtones between the cross and the lynching tree,
both places of execution in the ancient and modern worlds?

JAMES CONE, *THE CROSS AND THE LYNCHING TREE*

IRA BERLIN, a distinguished professor at the University of
Maryland, describes the African American experience as a series of
passages through which people transformed a previously foreign
and unknown place or land into a home. Through these series of
passages, the meaning of their experiences changed, and blackness

was continually redefined.[1] One of these passages was what is now known as the Great Migration. From roughly 1915 to 1970, over six million blacks migrated from the South to the North—more people than moved during the Gold Rush of the 1850s or the Dust Bowl migration in the 1930s. Isabel Wilkerson writes, "It was the first mass act of independence by a people who were in bondage in this country for far longer than they have been free."[2] And the country was never the same.

PUSH-AND-PULL FACTORS

Before the Great Migration, only 10 percent of blacks lived in the North, while the remaining 90 percent—or seven million—were in the South. Despite persecution, violence, and segregation, black persons seemed rooted in the southern land until a complex combination of push-and-pull factors triggered a migration: an average of five hundred blacks per day, and more than fifteen thousand per month, left the South until under one in five Americans of African descent remained in the South.[3]

World War I was one of the primary factors creating the migration and pulling southern blacks to the North. At the same time that many workers were called to the war, immigration into the United States significantly decreased, leading to a huge need for industrial workers—particularly those willing to work for low wages. You could earn four dollars a day picking cotton in the South, while in cities like Chicago you could make as much as seventy-five cents an hour working in a laundry, factory, restaurant, or hotel.[4]

Federal officials and northern industrialists added to the pull as well. The Labor Department created the Division of Negro Economics, while businesses sent representatives to the South to recruit laborers. In 1916 and 1917, Robert Sengstacke Abbott, publisher of the leading black newspaper, the *Chicago Defender*, began to publicly call on blacks to leave the South and to move north. Abbott set "the Great Northern

Drive," as it came to be called, for May 15, 1917. He persuaded railroads to offer discounted rates to groups of blacks migrating to Chicago, and he recruited white labor agents and black preachers to tour the South so they could recruit others. Black porters on the Illinois Central Railroad spread the word to help Abbott's mobilization efforts.[5]

Meanwhile in the South, African Americans were trapped in Jim Crow segregation and violence as well as the exploitative sharecropper system. Though they were no longer confined to one plantation, share-cropping farmers were frequently disappointed when it came time to settle up with the landowner.

In addition to the limited economic opportunities, blacks in the South faced great violence and harassment. From 1889 to 1929, someone was lynched or burned alive every four days. According to *The Tragedy of Lynching*, published in 1933, victims were lynched for alleged crimes such "stealing hogs, horse-stealing, poisoning mules, jumping labor contracts, suspected of killing cattle, boastful remarks . . . [and] trying to act like a white person." A total of sixty-six people were killed for supposedly insulting a white person.[6]

Other factors contributing to the Great Migration included indus-trialization: many black southerners were drawn to the industrial centers of the North in search of a better life. The Chicago Com-mission on Race Relations, created after World War I, asked migrants why they had left the South and come to Chicago. The answers varied greatly: "Some of my people were here . . . persuaded by my friends . . . to better my condition . . . more work . . . wife persuaded me . . . to get away from the South."[7]

Throughout this time white southerners themselves had an evolving relationship to the migration. Initially they retaliated and tried to stop those trying to leave with intimidation, "anti-enticement laws, controls on labor agents, and even legislation against hitchhiking."[8] These whites were desperate to understand why blacks were leaving while they were still so dependent on their labor. As black voting began to increase, however, the issue of school desegregation arose, and with that the desire to move blacks out of the South began to increase. As Aaron Henry, a leader of the civil rights movement in Mississippi, put it, "They wished we'd go back to Africa, but Chicago was close enough."[9]

Though migration was strong leading up to World War II, the economic growth that resulted from World War II brought on a new wave of migration that dwarfed the earlier migration. In total, between the early 1900s and 1970, six million African Americans relocated from the rural South to the cities of the North, Midwest, and West.

CHANGING DEMOGRAPHICS, OPPORTUNITIES, AND CULTURE

Due to the nature of the push-and-pull factors, the flow northward was to major metropolitan cities and industrial centers such as Chicago, Boston, Detroit, New York, Philadelphia, and Pittsburgh, and even smaller cities such as Hartford and Oakland. By 1960 nearly three-quarters of the black population in the United States lived in cities, and 90 percent of the population in the North was urban.[10] This was a massive shift as the center of black life and culture moved from rural to urban. The migration patterns were so clear that when the Great Migration had ended, you could tell where a black northerner's family was from based on where they had settled. One stream was along the Eastern Seaboard, another centered along the Mississippi, while another carried migrants to the West Coast.[11]

There is no doubt that greater freedom existed in the North than in the South—blacks could walk on sidewalks without moving for whites; they could vote; and they were allowed to sit in the front of the bus. There was certainly more economic opportunity as well. However, there was still great difficulty in the North. Job options were limited due to discrimination, and the jobs available were unstable. Eventually as the civil rights movement grew and the Fair Employment Practices Commission was established, discrimination in the work force declined from 1940 to 1960, and the number of blacks employed in white-collar jobs doubled.[12]

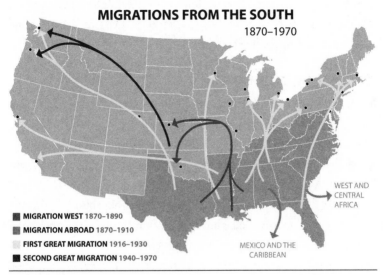

MIGRATIONS FROM THE SOUTH
1870–1970

■ **MIGRATION WEST** 1870–1890
■ **MIGRATION ABROAD** 1870–1910
■ **FIRST GREAT MIGRATION** 1916–1930
■ **SECOND GREAT MIGRATION** 1940–1970

WEST AND CENTRAL AFRICA

MEXICO AND THE CARIBBEAN

Figure 3. The great migration

Great concentrations of African Americans in cities led to a great awakening of black culture. As Ira Berlin writes, "[Blacks,] forced to create a city within a city, soon found excitement in the places where they could locate their own food, religion, and music."[13] The two most famous examples of these cultural centers were New York's Harlem and Chicago's Bronzeville, though most cities had their own version of these neighborhoods. Black music was one of the defining aspects of the cultural awakening that came from the Great Migration—and was one of the most influential on the nation.[14]

It was during this time that traditional spirituals turned into gospel music, and gospel and urban blues combined into rhythm and blues, made famous at the time by artists such as Ray Charles and Sam Cooke. It was also during this time that black music began to be packaged for white audiences.[15] Three of the greatest jazz musicians— Miles Davis, Thelonious Monk, and John Coltrane—were children of the Great Migration.[16] Many songs had explicit references to the Great Migration, including Blind Blake's "Detroit Bound Blues" and Bessie Smith's "Chicago Bound Blues." Duke Ellington's famous song "Take the 'A' Train" directed new migrants to Harlem with the line "You must take the 'A' Train to Sugar Hill / Way up in Harlem."[17]

RACISM IN THE NORTH

Migrants to the North found they were forced to confront racism there too, even if it showed itself in different ways. Not only employment restrictions but also housing segregation presented significant obstacles and contributed greatly to the current makeup and layout of America's cities today. For example, as the south side and west side of Chicago developed into "black neighborhoods," both suffered severe overcrowding and dilapidation. However, rather than expand the neighborhoods, Mayor Richard J. Daley of Chicago worked hard to maintain the lines. Rather than integrate neighborhoods to eliminate overcrowding in schools populated by black students, Daley created double shifts and temporary classrooms for those schools while nearby white schools sat half-empty.[18]

Expanding or integrating black neighborhoods was a difficult, if not impossible, proposal, given that white neighborhoods were protected by many customs and laws.

THE VALUE OF A HOME

The idea of homeownership is woven deep into the fabric of what it means to be American. In the 1946 Christmas classic *It's a Wonderful Life*, George Bailey implores his father to let him do something more important than working at the savings and loan. His father responds with sage wisdom to a naive child by saying: "You know, George, I feel that in a small way we are doing something important. Satisfying a fundamental urge. It's deep in the race for a man to want his own roof and walls and fireplace, and we're helping him get those things in our shabby little office."[19]

The elder Bailey calling homeownership a "fundamental urge" is a reflection of its importance in American society. Owning a home is deep in our collective consciousness and represents at least a partial fulfillment of the American dream.

One of the first threads woven into that American fabric came with the passage of President Abraham Lincoln's Homestead Act of 1862. Signed into law during the American Civil War, the Homestead Act stated that any "current or future citizens," with the submission of a ten-dollar application fee, could claim up to 160 acres of government land. After five continuous years of living on and cultivating the land, the citizen would be granted the title to it free. In all, the Homestead Act distributed 270 million acres of land between 1862 and 1986, when the final deed was handed out.[20] Though it was partly aimed at providing newly freed slaves a chance at claiming land of their own, the "current or future citizen" clause excluded former slaves from signing up for the first three years because they were barred from citizenship.

In the 1930s, homesteading and landownership gave way to a full push toward homeownership as part of President Franklin D. Roosevelt's New Deal legislation. The New Deal was designed to help Americans get out of poverty with programs such as social security and unemployment insurance. However, the New Deal programs excluded agriculture and domestic labor—employment sectors that were largely nonwhite. Thus a large percentage of African Americans and other nonwhites failed to benefit from this legislation.[21]

In June 1933, President Roosevelt signed into law an act that created the Home Owners' Loan Corporation (HOLC), aimed at refinancing mortgages to stem foreclosures in the aftermath of the Great Depression. A year later, the Federal Housing Authority (FHA) was created to provide federally approved homeowners' insurance. Before the FHA and HOLC, few Americans owned their home; we were primarily a nation of renters. With a down payment requirement of nearly 50 percent, and a repayment period ranging only from three to five years, most people could not afford to buy their own home. The FHA and HOLC changed that by introducing fixed-rate mortgages with a repayment period of fifteen years. Just between 1933 and 1936, HOLC provided over a million loans.[22] By 1960, 60 percent of Americans owned their houses—though this number still largely excluded African Americans.[23] One of the more powerful forces shaping this is what is now known as redlining.

REDLINING

Before being closed in 1936, HOLC was asked to conduct research on 239 cities and to create "residential security maps." These maps, devised in partnership with local realtors and lenders, were intended to indicate the level of risk associated with real-estate investments at a community level within each of the cities researched. With explicit guidance from the FHA, these maps provided the basis used by realtors and lenders to decide who qualified for low-interest mortgages and to which houses those mortgages could be applied.

On the FHA/HOLC maps, neighborhoods outlined in green were marked with an *A* and described as areas that "lacked a single foreigner or negro," while neighborhoods with blacks living in them were given a *D* rating and made ineligible for FHA backing.[24] *D* neighborhoods were outlined in red—and thus the term *redlining* was born.

As African Americans sought better lives outside overcrowded city centers, they found they were barred from receiving the same federal assistance as whites. Of the one million loans handed out by HOLC from 1933 to 1936, fewer than twenty-five thousand, or 2.5 percent, went to nonwhites. A portion of the guidelines released by the FHA read: "The Valuator should investigate areas surrounding the location to determine whether or not incompatible racial and social groups are present. . . . If a neighborhood is to retain stability it is necessary that properties shall continue to be occupied by the same social and racial classes. A change in social or racial occupancy generally leads to instability and a reduction in values."[25]

Have you ever wondered why America remains as segregated as it is, long after segregation in schools and public facilities was outlawed? The answer is simple: racial policies, to a large degree, directed, dictated, and determined the racial makeup of neighborhoods in America. One of the central arguments of this book, as we uncover the roots of injustice and privilege, is that the effects of state-sponsored racism in America are very much present today.

Beyond the FHA's racially biased policies, the 1924 Code of Ethics released by the National Association of Real Estate Board included this directive: "The Realtor should never be instrumental in introducing into a neighborhood . . . members of any race or nationality, or any individuals whose presence will clearly be detrimental to property values in that neighborhood."[26] Remarkably, this portion of the realtor guidebook was retained until 1974—two years after I was born.

Without access to federally backed mortgages, blacks were generally forced to stay within the rental market's redlined areas of town—what we typically now view as a ghetto—and they were therefore unable to accrue equity the way the majority of whites did during this time. The other option, for those who had enough money saved, was to buy through a private contractor. Ta-Nehisi Coates researched the situation in Chicago and found that 85 percent of all African American homebuyers bought on contract.[27]

In many neighborhoods private contractors used scare tactics to induce white families to sell their homes at reduced rates; then they resold them at double the price to blacks. For example, in 1961 a man named Clyde Ross—originally from Clarksdale, Mississippi—decided to move to North Lawndale in Chicago's west side. Before the Great Migration, the community had been predominantly white and middle to upper class. When Ross was rejected for an FHA mortgage, he bought a house from a private contractor. He paid $27,000 for a house the previous owner had purchased for $12,000 only six months earlier. The contract declared that the deed would stay in the hands of the seller until the loan had been fully satisfied, and if any of the loan payments were missed, the house would return to the seller's possession with no return of payments or Ross's deposit.

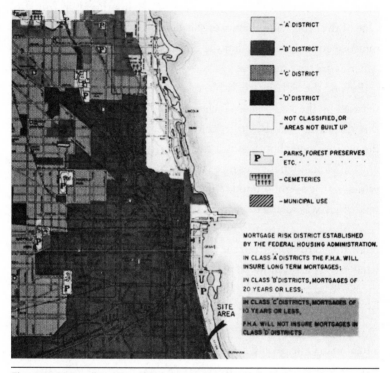

Figure 4. 1938 redline map of Chicago. Notice the similarity in comparison to the recent dot map showing segregation in America based on recent census data (figure 5). Many American cities still retain much of the shape of the redlined zones from earlier periods.

Thus private contract sales produced "all the responsibilities of home owning with all the disadvantages of renting."[28] Once one black family was evicted, the seller would repeat the process with a new black family, and so it would continue. In a 2009 interview, a Chicago housing attorney said of the exploitative lenders: "It was like people who like to go out and shoot lions in Africa. It was the same thrill . . . the thrill of the chase and the kill."[29]

This was the pattern of white flight. Fear of insecurity and the financial devaluation of houses after blacks moved into the neighborhood induced whites to sell their houses at low prices. Indeed the fear of communities declining became a self-fulfilling prophecy, because once a community became majority African American, outside investment and resources departed.

John McKnight, professor emeritus at Northwestern University and the person who popularized the term *redlining* for the historical practice and its relationship to the shape of communities and neighborhoods today, explains that redlining was "the mechanism that insured the real estate industry would continue to produce the ghetto."[30]

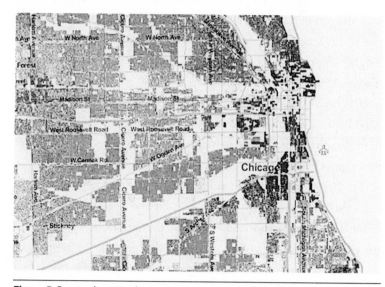

Figure 5. Recent dot map showing segregation in Chicago (https://demographics .virginia.edu/DotMap/index.html)

Chicago was not the only place this occurred. In Levittown, Pennsylvania—a picture of white suburban life—the first black family to move in was met by protestors and a burning cross. One neighbor commented that even though he knew they were probably nice, "every time I look at him I see $2,000 drop off the value of my house."[31]

Testifying before a US Commission on Civil Rights hearing in 1970, Adel Allen, a resident of Kirkwood, Missouri (a suburb of St. Louis), explained that their neighborhood went from thirty white families and one black family in 1962 to thirty black and two white families just eight years later. In the same time period, the police protection, street maintenance, trash services, and lighting declined significantly, while his tax payments remained constant.[32]

The practice of redlining was not outlawed until the Fair Housing Act was passed in 1968. By that time the damage had been done; redlining created disparate wealth and economic opportunities. Between 1983 and 2013, homeownership rates among whites were roughly 25 percent higher than among nonwhites.[33] Meanwhile, the median wealth of white families grew from $46,160 in 1963 to $134,230 in 2013, while African American wealth grew from $2,390 to $11,030, and Hispanic wealth grew to $13,730. In 1983, whites held eight times more wealth than African Americans, and in 2013 they enjoyed twelve times more wealth.[34]

The Great Migration and redlining set in motion much of what is reflected in the structure of our cities today and also set in place many of the demographic and economic issues that became the platform for the war on drugs.

The migration shaped so many aspects of American life—the layout of our cities, the nature of the civil rights movement past and present, the content of so much art and music.

It also partly explains why the region where I live—the Pacific Northwest—is one of the least diverse areas in the nation. Because the northward movement was largely to industrial centers, of which there were few in the Northwest at the time, there were not as many economic opportunities here as in other places. Oregon also had many exclusionary laws in place well into the 1900s, which discouraged people of color from coming and settling here.[35]

Diversity and segregation, like the Grand Canyon, are not random phenomena but are shaped by real decisions and real forces over long periods.

CONCLUSION

The Greek word *eschatos* simply means "last things." The word *eschatology* means the study of last things. When we talk about eschatology in the church, we are speaking with regard to the end times, or how the story of God will resolve.

One of the more specific pictures of last things is the worship of God's people before his throne, described in Revelation 7:9-10:

> After this I looked, and there before me was a great multitude that no one could count, from every nation, tribe, people and language, standing before the throne and before the Lamb. They were wearing white robes and were holding palm branches in their hands. And they cried out in a loud voice:
>
> > "Salvation belongs to our God,
> > who sits on the throne,
> > and to the Lamb."

We see that worship, or engaged relationship (the true nature of worship), is one of our ultimate ends. We are headed for a time when we will stand with members from every nation, tribe, people, and language as one unified people of God. In short, the chorus before God in heaven is a diverse one. It represents members from all of God's creation—a group of men and women representing all of the various peoples God created in his image.

In heaven, as on earth, there is horizontal diversity among God's people. The biblical language—"nation, tribe, people and language"—

implies racial diversity without using the word *race*. *Race* in its current usage, as we have seen, was a much later and arbitrary term developed to classify people not by language or nation but by color. It's arbitrary in the sense that it has fluid borders and categorizes people not based in any kind of biological difference other than appearance.

In the 1400s, when an accelerated racial view of people began, we turned horizontal diversity into vertical categories. Where God created variety, we established hierarchy, in which "we" (as white European descendants) are better than "them" (who look different than we do). There should be a connection between our theology with God and our ordering of society.

This hierarchical way of seeing people according to color is nowhere advocated in God's Word—not in the beginning and not at the end. It is a worldview that, like a word untimely spoken, has proved almost impossible to undo.

Over the centuries children were born into a world that slotted them in both spoken and unspoken ways into a hierarchy based on color; many of them internalized and propagated that same worldview to future generations until all peoples were categorized and labeled.

In the United States we no longer accept either slavery or legally enforced segregation based on color, but that doesn't mean we haven't inherited elements of the racial hierarchy that supported slavery and Jim Crow laws.

Race, as a way of seeing and categorizing people, is a paradigm with immense historical momentum. A boat does not stop immediately when it is throttled down, and its wake continues even longer. Likewise, race, racial bias, and racially constructed societal patterns don't immediately pass from memory when they are discredited. They linger in the shadows of our laws, in the ways society is represented in movies and music, and—in a deeper and more profound manner—in the ways we perceive ourselves as privileged or not.

As Christians and as the church, our north star, however, remains the kingdom of God and its values rather than the ways of worldly empires. Our end is radical horizontal diversity reflecting the beauty of God's image and the variety of his creativity. We are destined for singing shoulder to shoulder with brothers and sisters beholding not a divisive hierarchy of worth but the glory of the One who created and unifies us.

The move from a vertical hierarchy of race to standing in a picture of horizontal diversity is our biblical trajectory. Anything that impedes this move to unity is not of God. Do not mistake values that keep us apart as biblical. Subtle forms of racial bias within us lead to feelings of superiority on one hand and self-hatred on the other. They blind us to the glory of God, our equal creation in his image, and, ultimately, destroy our collective song.

How have Christianity and racism been able to coexist so often and in so many places?

The answer surely must be that there are forces or desires we cherish more deeply than unity.

In part two we will look at some of the brokenness in our aspirations, theology, and practice, with the hope of recapturing a vision of equality within the kingdom of God.

PART II

EQUALITY AND THE KINGDOM OF GOD

FIVE

THE ARISTOCRATIC ITCH

> Christians are located inside nations and modern nation-states,
> which means that Christian theology is also located inside a
> constricting configuration of the social imagination. . . . The
> confinement expresses a style of imagining social reality.
>
> **WILLIE JAMES JENNINGS,** *THE CHRISTIAN IMAGINATION*

TRUTH BE TOLD, whether we realize it or not, we all harbor romantic notions of aristocracy. Though we claim equality as a cultural value, there is a part of us that dreams of leisure, luxury, comfort, power, and the freedom to do whatever we want.

Don't believe me?

In 2011 *Downton Abbey*, the famous television series about an aristocratic manor and the various personalities who inhabit it, set the Guinness World Record for highest critical ratings for a television show.[1]

In the 2015 music video for Taylor Swift's song "Wildest Dreams," Swift is cast as a golden-age film actress somewhere in colonial Africa (there's not a single black person in the video). The video was criticized harshly by Viviane Rutabingwa and James Kassaga Arinaitwean in an NPR segment for its disregard of the brutality of that era in African history: "They should have wondered how Africans would react. This nostalgia that privileged white people have for colonial Africa is awkwardly confusing to say the least and offensive to say the most." They continue, "Colonialism was neither romantic nor beautiful. It was exploitative and brutal."[2]

Swift's romanticizing of a world where white people sat atop the world as aristocrats or adventurers in societies that functioned on the backs of laboring people of color isn't a new phenomenon. Hollywood has been romanticizing the manors, estates, society balls, and beautiful gowns of the Old South in films such as *Gone with the Wind* for decades. The Old South was hardly a romantic place for the slaves who built, maintained, and farmed those manors. The historic and racial exploitation of masses of men and women shouldn't serve as a backdrop for an aristocratic movie character we're meant to fall in love with. It should be deeply troubling when we're subtly led to respect a character who is exploiting, or complicit in the exploitation of, masses of men and women along racial lines.

Our fascination with aristocracy extends beyond simply romanticizing culture. We also have an enormous number of aristocratic heroes and heroines. Many of the great thinkers we revere were from the European nobility: Montaigne, Hume, Erasmus. These men had the means, the education, and the discretionary time to devote to study and reflection and philosophy. Much of Western achievement and innovation has originated within the elite class.

In a (not so) subtle way, when we contemplate our geniuses of art, science, and philosophy, we are almost always venerating members of an elite class. In many ways, this might be part of human nature, but we like to see ourselves in them. We want the same stability and ability to study while other people take care of the more mundane aspects of our lives. We see ourselves in Downton Abbey.

What is nobility? This elite class? Where did it come from? Why does it still hold so much power over our imagination?

THE AMERICAN DREAM

Among the beautiful things about America are the many rags-to-riches stories embedded in our history. When America was founded in the late 1700s, much of Europe was still living in a frozen socio-economic structure, with one king at the top and peasants at the bottom. But throughout America in the 1800s, unless you were enslaved or a member of a minority, many Americans were free to engage in business or commerce. Through hard work and the Puritan work ethic, our society allowed many Americans to change their socioeconomic status and move upward.

This might not seem so revolutionary now, but it was then, because white Americans had migrated from Europe, a culture deeply entrenched in aristocracy, or "peerage." Peerage is an invitation-only system engineered to keep outsiders from cracking it. It was designed to perpetuate inequality so monarchs could maintain order and continue to exercise power.

The system of nobility was created by feudal monarchs in the Middle Ages as a way of rewarding local influential leaders and maintaining their loyalty. In the United Kingdom the nobility developed slowly, in a rather hodgepodge fashion, over four hundred years, from the eleventh to the fifteenth century. The earl was the first rank of British peerage. Earls were responsible for collecting taxes, deciding justice in local courts, ruling their shire, and leading the king's army when the kingdom was at war. Over time, monarchs added more titles and distinctions to give themselves more political leverage. These are the British ranks of peerage in descending order: duke (duchess), marquess (marchioness), earl (countess), viscount (viscountess), and baron (baroness).

There are only two ways to become a noble: through birth or through the monarch's grant of a title. That's it. If your father wasn't a noble and you didn't happen to be friends with a king or queen, your chances of becoming nobility were nil. So a poor boy born in London in the 1800s had a far smaller chance of achieving any upward mobility during his lifetime than a poor boy born in Boston, simply because in London the peerage system was designed to keep him from ascending in the social order.

There was a cultural element to this as well, beyond merely the structure of peerage: Americans *felt* (and still feel) they were all peers and equals, despite their heritage. As recently as 1931, John Truslow Adams, an American historian, wrote, "I once had an intelligent young Frenchman as a guest in New York, and after a few days I asked him what struck him most among his new impressions. Without hesitation, he replied, 'The way that everyone of every sort looks you right in the eye, without a thought of inequality.'"[3]

Dreaming of or imagining a better state, a fairy-tale ending, or the desire to be a part of royalty has always been a human aspiration or dream. Isn't this what we see in Charles Dickens's *Great Expectations*? The difference is that, in America, it became codified as an expectation and a right.

But as noble as the ideals of the American dream are, the idea that "it's easy" to write your own rags-to-riches story is a myth, and it always has been. It has never really been true that *anyone* in America can become *anything* they want to be. While we all know stories of just that, these are, more often, the exception and not the rule. There were more poor, nonslaving white people in the South than there were slaving plantation owners.[4] And as we will see later in this book, one of the fastest-growing, most disillusioned segments of America, with a quickly declining life expectancy, are poor white Americans.

Known as the poor white, or poor whites of the South, this underclass was actually prevented from entering the middle class by the institution of slavery. They often took out their disillusionment and hostility on the blacks of the South rather than on the ruling elites who created structures such as the poll tax designed to keep them in their social class as much as to exclude the black vote.

That said, there is enough validity to the American dream that it has always held a firm grip on our consciousness and psyche. In short, we believe that if we play our cards right, and with a little bit of luck, we can reach a level of financial security that will allow us to do everything we want and achieve our dreams. Anything less than this feels like a failure.

Did you catch that phrase in the last paragraph: "everything we want"? We have an idealized picture of a life of leisure. The picture borrows elements from aristocracy—both from history and from movies and television. The American dream is more connected to aristocracy than we realize.

Doesn't it seem odd that in America, where one of our closest-held values is equality, we so revere and romanticize this unashamedly stratified system of inequality? Perhaps the American dream isn't as American as we think it is. Sociologists used to say Americans have an aristocracy of class—which used to mean money but nowadays means power, status, or education. The small group of people who controlled the trajectory of the world, and often the very lives of peasants, have so captured our imagination that somehow we have turned them into the good guys. They're our heroes, the people we're trying to become.

We love the character of Tom, the family chauffeur on *Downton Abbey*, because even though he rails against the oppression of the ruling class, he is able to transcend his poverty and station and join them. And we *love* the nobility for welcoming him into their family and think: *That's how I would be if I were noble. I would be accepting and loving and gracious.* The other side of that story is, of course, that while they were loving and accepting and gracious, the family continued to spend money on lavish parties, expensive clothes, and rich food while an entire household of people lived and worked as servants one floor below. But we tend not to identify with the peasants in the show (even though statistically most of us would definitely have been born peasants, not nobles). There is a strange connection between our human aspirations and entertainment, where entertainment not only reflects many of our desires but also shapes and reinforces many of those same aspirations. And in this way, not only is it self-perpetuating, but it is also one of the mechanisms for cutting such a deep cultural groove.

Subtly, my desire for virtue is usually connected to and embedded in *privilege*. Somehow I'm aiming for and only think I'm going to be comfortable with privilege, which becomes problematic when I'm confronted with the reality that *privilege and equality don't go together*.

PRIVILEGE AND THE KINGDOM OF GOD

The Old Testament prophets often referred to a group's misuse of privilege as the reason the group was being judged. Jesus gave up his privilege, and he calls us to do the same. Philippians 2:5-8 says:

In your relationships with one another, have the same mindset
as Christ Jesus:

Who, being in very nature God,
   did not consider equality with God
   something to be used to his own advantage;

rather, he made himself nothing
   by taking the very nature of a servant,
   being made in human likeness.

And being found in appearance as a man,
   he humbled himself
   by becoming obedient to death—
   even death on a cross!

Jesus did not strive for or cling to privilege, and because we are called to be like him, neither should we.

Privilege, or what we do with it, is something God cares dearly about.

On one hand, we want to feel like we're really good with justice and race and generosity. On the other hand, just beneath the surface, all of our significant dials are tuned into affluence and ease. It is common for me to talk to people who want to pursue justice but only after they have taken care of themselves first. In the Gospels we see that this was a common response that Jesus encountered. Humans seemingly have a natural tendency to want to make the purpose of God's good news the promotion and protection of our comfort.

The word *aristocracy* simply means "the rule of the best." Aristocracy might seem desirable, but is it truly the best? The idea of aristocracy rings hollow when we compare it to Jesus' claim that in his kingdom "the last will be first, and the first will be last" (Matthew 20:16).

The kingdom of God was a hallmark of Jesus' preaching and teaching. In fact, "kingdom of God" or "kingdom of heaven" is mentioned eighty-five times in the New Testament.

When Jesus preached his message about the kingdom, it was incredibly disruptive, so disruptive that the establishment had him executed. He came into direct opposition with a powerful group of people who were more invested in protecting their influence and position than in hearing truth.

Anthony Bradley, chair of religious studies at King's College in New York City, says, "Christians tend simply to align themselves with secular and idolatrous ideologies, and they do this without integrating fully into their thinking the ways in which kingdom priorities ought to arrange a Christian's perspective on the society by holding love, human dignity, and solidarity in healthy tension."[5]

THE EMPIRE

In 1978, American theologian Walter Brueggemann wrote a book called *The Prophetic Imagination*. It was a fresh look at the Old Testament, highlighting the ability of the prophets—rather than the society that was protecting the status quo—to imagine or dream of how things could be if society were structured according to God's will. Brueggemann states that "the empire" stands in opposition to God's vision for society or the kingdom. He defines empire as "any concentration of wealth or power that means to impose itself as a dominant definer of reality."[6]

Privilege, being situated comfortably within the empire, is easy to see when other people have it, but it's often hard to recognize when we have it. If our imagination is captured by the empire rather than by Christ, we will defend the empire—even if we are inadvertently defending it against Christ.

Says Brueggemann, "Sometimes the church itself takes the form of empire when it insists on absolute governance and absolute opinion making."[7]

In other words, if the church becomes an empire unto itself, a self-interested institution concerned with its own power and influence (as the temple had become in Jesus' day), it is capable of slipping into direct opposition to the kingdom of God—the very thing it is supposed to be nurturing, spreading, and protecting.

When we allow ourselves to be sucked into believing the empire's narrative, we succumb to what Brueggemann calls "the royal consciousness," or the "groupthink" of the empire. There is a danger that it will begin to inform and shape our behavior and expectations in relationship to ourselves, others, our surroundings, our definition of success, and God. As Brueggemann writes, "The royal consciousness is the dominant social consciousness of a culture that is shaped by and ultimately supports the ideals and actions of the empire. It is important that we understand the overall consciousness of our culture so that we can see how it has compromised our understanding of God, ourselves and our relationship with other people."[8]

Our imagination has a powerful ability to shape both our perception of reality and the reality that we actually bring into being. If our picture of the ideal life is defined, in part, by Taylor Swift and pop culture, it will powerfully shape our values, our goals, and the methods we employ to pursue them.

If we were thinking prophetically about what God would desire, according to his kingdom principles, what would we imagine or dream? "Imagination is inherently subversive," writes Brueggemann.

"It undermines and calls into question all of the things that we think are settled and that we've reduced to packaged certitudes." If empire is simply a concentration of wealth and power that imposes a different set of values from God's, what would we identify as the areas where empire is steering us away from justice and right relationship with others and toward an amassing of privilege, a protection of that privilege, and a pseudotheology to justify and undergird our pursuit of the American dream?

I don't know about you, but I feel like I'm steeped in a culture with a will toward aristocracy. When Jesus says, "If you have one coat, give your second coat away" (see Matthew 5:40), aristocracy would say, "Two coats is a great place to be on your way to three. And sooner or later you'll have enough coats to allow you to wear whatever you want whenever you want. And that person with only one coat? They're not disadvantaged; they're just reaping the consequences of their lack of a work ethic."

Have we adopted a desire to be the new aristocracy without calling it that? Do we have a worldview that allows us not to have to deal with the moral implications of the aristocratic enterprise? Is the church itself a vehicle of the empire, an institution that perpetuates the dominant worldview and doesn't allow it to be called into question?

I once preached out of the book of Amos. Amos is an uncompromising prophetic voice. I felt convicted and began to question what my role is as a truth teller or a voice disruptive to the status quo. I looked at our associate pastor and commented that if any sermon had the potential to blow up our congregation, this one might.

In this book God himself calls Amos to bring a disruptive message so the establishment can change and be redeemed. Rather than responding with humility and remorse, the empire doubles down on its message and attempts to push the prophet out.

God often brings a word from the outside to call his people to faithful living.

My driving goal in leadership is to bring people together, establish a healthy culture, disciple the community, and mobilize them to serve each other and their surrounding world. As a teacher, I realize I am supposed to take up the mantle of Amos—to carry that prophetic message. But the prophetic message doesn't often bring unity, stabilize culture, or mobilize people to listen. To address difficult times in the life of our community or nation is to elicit a strong response.

The prophetic word explodes things.

THE PROPHETIC VOICE

Brueggemann alluded to this once, in a conversation with a classroom of students at Kilns College: "Make a list of all the things that you cannot talk about in the church that we ought to be talking about. Nobody is opposed to soup kitchens and tutoring programs in disadvantaged schools. But if you [try to bring up] class orientation of public schools or the systemic causes of poverty, you can't talk about this stuff, because we are so acclimated to the American capitalist system."[9]

As much as it pains me to say it—because I want to believe my church is an authentic, fearless community capable of rigorous thought—there are things in the community of Antioch here in Bend, Oregon (and many other evangelical communities) we don't want to talk about and don't want to let any of our leaders talk about. Think about it: gun control, party politics, abortion, LGBTQ issues, US militarism, universal health care, wealth disparity, the welfare system— are these subjects we can comfortably discuss from the pulpit? If I preached about them, many people would get uncomfortable (no matter what I said), and a lot of people would begin to wonder if I've become a crazy liberal, or perhaps a crazy conservative.

We don't want anything or anyone disrupting or subverting the religious climate that allows us to get along by not talking about things that we find challenging or that confront our value system. If we did, those in economic, political, or religious power would suddenly feel like their control was slipping away. But by avoiding these difficult and uncomfortable issues, we reinforce privilege.

So, as leaders, we are pressured to avoid those things. The same pressure was applied to Jesus. The word he brought was so disruptive to the religious leaders of his day that they went to the other empire—the Roman Empire—and persuaded it that he was dangerous. They conspired and killed him as king of the Jews.

The righteous establishment will always say, "God is with us." I want to believe that God is with Antioch and working in Antioch, but the simple reality is that God is *not* always with or pleased with the people who claim he is with them.

What do we do when we realize we all want the status quo?

The prophetic voice explodes the status quo. It refuses to allow the dominant, wealthy, powerful empire to claim ultimate authority over reality.

It's subversive.

Radical.

Disruptive.

And when the prophetic voice is functioning the way it's supposed to, in our biblical tradition, the empire seeks to silence it. The scary thing is, to echo Brueggemann, "sometimes the church itself takes the form of empire." As hard as it is to believe (or perhaps it isn't), I've discovered this to be true as I have attempted to open conversation about racial justice in my church as well as in the wider Christian community.

The empire is out there. It is real. It might even be—whether you understand it or not—the culture you exist in. And I hope we would always have ears to hear and eyes to see what the Spirit is saying, that we would be willing to do what Paul said and, instead of banning conversations, to test the spirits, hold on to what is good, and reject what is bad.

As hard as it might be, we should realize that discipleship—following Jesus, picking up our cross daily—implies a willingness to lay down power, use privilege for others' benefit, and pay the cost of faithful obedience to God. As a disciple, I am committed to his vision—not only for my life but also for the society and culture I may help to shape. Is this not why Jesus taught the disciples to pray, "Thy kingdom come, thy will be done, on earth as it is in heaven" (Matthew 6:10 KJV)?

GROUP RIGHTEOUSNESS

Group righteousness arises within the empire when we all decide we belong to a "good group," and because it's a good group, we are immune to criticism. Since we're immune, we can continue to reinforce our belief that we're the good group and we're good guys. Then, anytime a prophetic word reaches us, we're already convinced it is for someone else.

That is what happened when Jesus confronted the Pharisees. They were convinced they were the good guys, and they couldn't help but feel that Jesus was being harsh and had chosen the wrong bad guys. After all, shouldn't Caesar and Rome be the bad guys? So they pushed Jesus out.

There are many people who will always want to return to the time when America was great. But was there ever a time when America was a wonderful place for *everyone*? As I saw on a Facebook meme recently: "Why do people romanticize the 1950s? Like calm down, we still have milkshakes and racism." Can't we look to the future and dream of something better instead? And why do we find it such bad form for a pastor to criticize America?

I remember the first time I spoke on immigration at Antioch. We were still less than two years old as a community and fragile. What I said didn't even hint at politics—just the need to welcome the stranger and love the foreigner—but twenty people left. Speaking biblical truth can be costly when our ears have been attuned to what a political party or the world says about truth.

It is a bad idea to bring up those subjects only if the purpose of the church has shifted to preserving the stability of the empire and not disrupting our interests.

If we can't even be honest about the history of our country, then we have somehow bestowed ourselves with "group righteousness," which means we're the good guys and anyone who is questioning our history is questioning us. If we're righteous, the questioner must be bad, and we refuse to listen to anything they have to say. If someone is going to speak prophetic words, obviously it must not be to us, because we're the good guys.

What if we are more focused on our net worth or our retirement funds than civil rights for other American citizens? Would that mean that wealth and security are more important to us than justice?

What if we are more focused on the safety of our communities than on the equity in sentencing or the justice system? Would that mean safety and comfort are more important than fairness or the rights of others?

Inadvertently, we can go from agents faithfully living out the kingdom of God to citizens protecting the status quo, protecting the establishment, protecting our *power*. To the degree we do, we have become the empire.

What would happen if we were so receptive to the disruptive message of God that if and when God disciplined us, we caught ourselves early and quickly enough to change direction?

"Rich and righteous," as defined by religious adherence and ritual, go together more easily than "rich and just," as defined by loving of neighbor and sacrifice. As Timothy Keller, a pastor and *New York Times*–bestselling author, says, "Any neglect shown to the needs of the members of the vulnerable is not called merely a lack of mercy or charity, but a violation of justice."[10]

GROWNUP CONVERSATIONS

I remember being a kid and having a hunger for grownups' conversations, but when I was around, the adults changed the subject to protect my innocent ears. I remember being frustrated and wanting to say (though I lacked this vocabulary), "I have a thirst for knowledge. I care about truth. No matter how scary or complex it is, I want to be in the grownup conversation, not sheltered from it."

When we turn on the evening news and see stories such as the death of Eric Garner, the mass shooting in Charleston, and the number of grand jury acquittals of police officers who have shot unarmed young men of color, I think we find ourselves hungry for the adult conversation. We're ready for a long, deep talk about race, history, privilege, laws, systems, and structures. I truly believe that if we had our choice, we would not want our Christian leaders, reporters, and fellow church members trying to shout down honest dialogue or to steer the conversation away to protect our illusions.

N. T. Wright, one of the world's leading Bible scholars, writes:

> What you do in the present—by painting, preaching, singing, sewing, praying, teaching, building hospitals, digging wells, campaigning for justice, writing poems, caring for the needy, loving your neighbor as yourself—will last into God's future. These activities are not simply ways of making the present life a little less beastly, a little more bearable, until the day when we leave it behind altogether. They are part of what we may call building for God's kingdom.[11]

There are some very difficult conversations regarding race and privilege in which the Western evangelical church needs to engage. They will be messy. They will be challenging. They will confront us with our own biases, assumptions, and "royal consciousness." But I think we are neglecting our sacred duty as prophets if we avoid them, and I don't want us to be guilty of supporting and defending the empire against the kingdom of God. And, more important, I am eager for us to live out our divine mandate to continue to discover and build God's kingdom.

One of the grownup conversations we must not shy away from is race. Race isn't just a good cause but a necessary one.

Race isn't just a deeply troubling issue from our past but a very complicated issue and sin in the present.

Racism is much more complex and subtle than we think, and it involves all of us.

And true biblical love is made manifest in our willingness to lay down privilege in order to help others in need or to redress inequity and injustice.

SIX

DOES JUSTICE BELONG IN OUR GOSPEL CONVERSATION?

If you believe what you like in the Gospels, and reject what you don't like, it is not the gospel you believe, but yourself.

SAINT AUGUSTINE

I WAS RECENTLY IN A MEETING, on the thirteenth floor of a New York high-rise, with Christian African American leaders. The topic of religious rights and their decline in many sectors of American society was debated. Specifically, the conversation centered on Christian colleges and their freedom to institute codes of conduct according to their biblical convictions. The growing challenge to religious liberty has been a cause for great alarm among many evangelicals. In this particular gathering, the bigger debate was on the push many white evangelical leaders were giving to African American leaders, and the African American church, to join them in fighting for religious rights. The conversation was both unexpected and telling.

Many of the leaders present wondered how white evangelicals expected them to put boots on the ground for this felt urgency, when many of those same evangelicals have never marched with the African American church for the full realization of civil rights. To this group, the hypocrisy was obvious.

One of the more interesting challenges in talking about justice is the false dichotomy that persists within evangelicalism, which sees the gospel as being distinct from societal concerns. From such a position, one can't help but view justice and equality as secondary, or even tertiary, values at best.

This is no small thing!

If the *center* of our faith doesn't speak to justice, then it becomes easy to ignore or lose sight of it amid life's day-to-day challenges.

As someone deeply concerned with the gospel and the authority of Scripture, I am convinced that in modern history we have misunderstood both.

I hope you can read the next few chapters slowly enough to catch the aha moment and the radical implications of realizing that the problem with our gospel is that it has been *too cross centered.*

Sound heretical?

It's not.

Read on to the end of this chapter and you'll see what I mean.

THE EVOLUTION OF OUR UNDERSTANDING OF JUSTICE

Over the last decade, I've had the privilege of watching as the conversation regarding justice in the church—both in the United States and abroad—has undergone radical transformation. When I was in graduate school and early in my ministry, talking about justice raised suspicion from my fellow evangelicals. Even more recently, when we began The Justice Conference, there were large Christian organizations whose boards of directors debated whether they could be affiliated with something whose title contained the divisive word *justice.* It's almost hard to imagine now, because the conversation has moved incredibly fast. I no longer find churches or pastors reacting negatively to the word *justice* or to the idea that we should be involved in addressing injustice in the world today. This is a significant first step toward understanding justice in God's economy: justice isn't just a good thing but a *necessary* thing.

Although most pastors and Christian leaders will readily embrace the ethical implications of justice today, they quickly become defensive if the justice conversation is allowed anywhere near our understanding of the gospel. I believe there is a second part of transformation that still needs to be realized with regard to the concept of justice and our understanding of the Christian gospel—or the "good news."

I understand the reasoning of the cautious pastors: Justice, which many Christians connect to the concept of good works, cannot be allowed to affect our understanding of the gospel because, as Paul states, "it is by grace you have been saved, through faith—and this is not from yourselves, it is the gift of God—not by works, so that no one can boast" (Ephesians 2:8-9). The gospel doesn't include works; therefore it doesn't include justice. This argument only holds if *justice* is simply synonymous with *works*.

It's not.

ON WORDS AND DINOSAURS

Words have meaning. They are descriptive, as I once taught my daughters using the word *dinosaur*—which literally means "terrible lizard." Words point us in one direction or another. When we don't want to do something, we argue about semantics, or the meaning of a word.

Something interesting happened in the history of the American church in the late 1800s, culminating in the 1910s and 1920s. A rift emerged between those who focused on addressing societal ills and those who focused on saving souls. Over time, each side was tied to a theological leaning. The "practical works of love" side became connected with liberal theology, while the preaching of Jesus Christ and the need for personal salvation was connected to conservative theology. As this rift deepened in the 1900s, as happens in any conflict, the two sides polarized.

The result in conservative evangelicalism was what theologian John Stott has called "the Great Reversal." This term was applied to the strange reversal of many Christian strands from their historical acts of social engagement—acts of charity, the building of hospitals, the abolition of slavery, and more. Suspicious and fearful of being associated with liberal theology, whole groups of Christians came to largely avoid work to redress worldly injustices or social ills.

This trend was exacerbated by the emergence of dispensational theology, with its emphasis on end times, which became increasingly popular in evangelical circles through the 1900s. The view of end times associated with dispensationalism is called premillennialism. Premillennialism entails the belief that life on earth will get progressively worse right up until the second coming of Christ. Those who embrace this theological view call attention to two world wars (and other smaller conflicts across the globe since 1945) and the rebirth of the Israeli nation-state to bolster their position. They also point to the increased number of Bible translations, which have reduced the number of people groups yet to hear of Jesus. Within the American experience, further support is found in our slide from a Christian to a post-Christian nation. For premillennialists, all of these events underscore the imminent end of the age.

Also inherent in this belief system (which was popularized a generation ago by the hugely successful Left Behind series of Christian novels) is the certainty that God's future plans for this creation are its annihilation and that our eternal destiny is in another place, heaven. So Christ's imminent return is not in order to usher in the fulfillment of his reign on earth or to complete the redemption and restoration of all things begun during the incarnation, crucifixion, and resurrection. Rather, he will return in order to take us away from a creation for which he has no further use.

Obviously, this view has significant implications for one's understanding of the gospel and of evangelism. For many evangelicals, the gospel begins and ends with saving human souls.

A favorite illustration among evangelicals who hold this view is that of a sinking *Titanic*. If the *Titanic* is sinking, the urgent priority should be getting as many people on the lifeboats as possible (thus saving them), and it would be foolish to waste time polishing the handrails on the staircases (addressing societal ills). This made perfect sense the first time someone made this argument to me in my early twenties.

But the question is whether the *Titanic* is sinking. Is the premillennial view correct? Because if the *Titanic* is not sinking, then it remains imperative to keep the ship seaworthy and to continue fulfilling the duties given us by the captain.

Dispensational theology's legacy has been, in part, to create a subtle fear that not only is social justice of secondary concern to our Christian mission but talking about it is also a dangerous logical fallacy that may start us down a slippery slope, with the potential to hollow out our understanding of Christian mission.

A THOUSAND GENERATIONS

Far too often we have speculated on the timing of Jesus' return—something that he seemingly encouraged us not to do (Mark 13:32). There's a big difference in how we approach something when there's a sense of urgency versus when there's a lot of time. If we have a lot of time left with kids in the home, we plan differently from the way we plan if we have less than a year left with them at home. A young and healthy person sees life a lot differently than someone with terminal cancer. Likewise, if I expect Jesus to come back in my lifetime, it greatly changes my focus from what it would be if Jesus were coming back in one thousand years.

When God gave the Ten Commandments, he made a telling—but oft-neglected—declaration that he would punish children for the sins of parents to the third and fourth generation of those who hated him, but would show love to a thousand generations of those who love him and keep his commands. If my obedience to Christ could literally lead to divine blessing on *a thousand generations* after me, how might that affect my sense of time and priority? And if obedience to God's commands is supposed to be a part of fulfilling his will on earth as it is in heaven, might not my Christian obedience lead to priorities of restorative justice that would over time help things on earth better approximate what they will be in the age to come, when every tongue and tribe will worship at the throne of Christ?

It's because of this understanding, encouraged by the biblical text, that racial reconciliation—one of the ways in which love of neighbor is manifested—has become a central priority in my Christian faith.

A proper understanding of both justice and the nature of the gospel shows us that they are inextricably intertwined.

WHAT DOES JUSTICE HAVE TO DO WITH THE GOSPEL?

The book of Isaiah is filled with discussions of justice, injustice, and God's impending discipline for Israel's lack of obedience. It can be a lot to take in, but Isaiah 59:14-17 is very illustrative:

> So justice is driven back,
>   and righteousness stands at a distance;
> truth has stumbled in the streets,
>   honesty cannot enter.
> Truth is nowhere to be found,
>   and whoever shuns evil becomes a prey.
>
> The LORD looked and was displeased
>   that there was no justice.
> He saw that there was no one,
>   he was appalled that there was no one to intervene;
> so his own arm achieved salvation for him,
>   and his own righteousness sustained him.
> He put on righteousness as his breastplate,
>   and the helmet of salvation on his head;
> he put on the garments of vengeance
>   and wrapped himself in zeal as in a cloak.

The first thing we can distill from this passage is a definition of justice. The passage begins by using *justice* and *righteousness* as synonyms in a format called Hebrew parallelism. In this format, a second phrase underscores and furthers what is said directly prior so that, in an oral culture, an audience will more fully understand the force of a stated truth. For the oral culture, this is equivalent to using boldface and italics.

There are over thirty-four places where *justice* and *righteousness* are used synonymously in Scripture. For example, Proverbs 8:20: "I walk in the way of righteousness, along the paths of justice." The relationship of the two words is strong; when originally used in the English translations of the Bible, they meant the same thing—roughly, the right relationship between God, self, others, and creation.

There is a misunderstanding associated with many contemporary translations. The Greek word *dikaiosyne* is variously translated as "righteousness" or "justice." Where it is translated "righteousness," we tend to infer that the passage is talking about moral purity; when it's translated "justice," we think of right relationships, fairness, and equality. But the Greek of the New Testament had just this single word, and its usage almost invariably involved all of these concepts rolled into one. This subtle false dichotomy comes into sharper view when we look at Spanish translations of the Bible. There is no Spanish word for "righteousness," so, like the Greek text, it uses one word to cover the large space of our right relationship with God and others. That word is *justicia*.

When Jesus says, in the eighth Beatitude, "Blessed are those who are persecuted because of righteousness, for theirs is the kingdom of heaven" (Matthew 5:10), he is referring to more than personal moral purity; he is attacking systems of injustice that tend to produce persecution. And Jesus' call to "seek first his kingdom and his righteousness, and all these things will be given to you as well" (Matthew 6:33) commands disciples not only to seek moral purity but to pursue integrity and right relationship in all aspects of life—between themselves and God, between themselves and others, and between themselves and the rest of God's creation.

The King James and the New King James Versions translate the well-known clause "the righteous person will live by his faithfulness" from the book of Habakkuk as "the just shall live by his faith." With a correct understanding of these words, we can see there is really no difference between the two—it is all *justicia*. But if we've grown up with an individualized, limited understanding of righteousness, then the *felt* difference between "the righteous will walk by faith" and "the just will walk by faith" is striking.

PRIMARY JUSTICE

Returning to Isaiah 59, we find that the chapter provides another way of understanding justice, making it parallel (equivalent) to the truth: "Justice is driven back, . . . truth has stumbled in the streets" (Isaiah 59:14). Justice and truth have often been defined in relation to each other. We tend to understand truth a little more intuitively. Philosophers have defined it simply as corresponding to reality, or "what is." Truth is a universal category, meaning it exists outside us, doesn't care what I think about it or whether I know or understand it. Truth and reality are cold, indifferent, and immovable.

Likewise, justice is a universal category. It refers to the moral sphere, or what "ought to be." It doesn't care whether I like it, whether I know it, or whether I understand it. At all times, in the mind of God there exists an idea of what ought to be.

Justice is multifaceted, and the various aspects of justice are sometimes difficult to distinguish and grasp. Nicholas Wolterstorff makes a helpful distinction between two basic elements of justice. The first is what he calls primary justice—when things are as they ought to be.[1] In Genesis, when God created and declared that it was good, it was because it matched his plan for creation. As any artist would, God had an idea of what he wanted to create, and the creation reflected his glory. This was as it ought to be. We still see instances of primary justice today, like the love of a mother for her child.

Primary justice is what the Hebrew word *shalom* denotes—peace and flourishing, as in a well-watered garden.

The second facet of justice is restorative justice. *Restorative justice* refers to all of the actions and efforts undertaken to make right the broken, bent, or perverted relationships in the world today. When Adam and Eve sinned, the world became broken. One of the more descriptive ways of picturing sin came to me when I read C. S. Lewis's *Out of the Silent Planet*. In describing humans who were from the silent planet (because of sin), the untainted creatures of Mars ended up using the term *bent*, as they had no word for sin. The idea that we are bent—that is, we are not in the condition we were in the garden when God created us—is a helpful picture. Therefore, restorative justice can be seen as the re-bending work of God, returning things back to the way he intended them to be.

Any time we seek to realign a particular situation or relationship, bringing it back to a state of primary justice, we are engaged in restorative justice. So restorative justice includes acts of Christian charity, and it incorporates the best aspects of criminal justice as well. It also entails much, much more—including all that goes into establishing and maintaining right relationships within society, or what we call social justice. As Gustavo Gutiérrez writes, "To preach the universal love of the Father is inevitably to go against all injustice, privilege, oppression, or narrow nationalism."[2] It is impossible to recognize this truth and not deal with the injustices stemming from race relations.

If we return to Isaiah, we see the continuation of what God is declaring to the people through the prophet:

> The LORD looked and was displeased
>   that there was no justice.
> He saw that there was no one,
>   he was appalled that there was no one to intervene;
> so his own arm achieved salvation for him,
>   and his own righteousness sustained him. (Isaiah 59:15-16)

After God led the Israelites out of slavery, gave them the law, led them into the Promised Land, sent them the leaders or "judges" to rescue them, gave them kings, and even sent prophets—still, there was no one who could satisfactorily ensure there would be justice in the land. So God intervenes, we're told, with his very arm, to achieve salvation. These verses are allusions to the Messiah, or God's incarnation in Jesus.

Reading Isaiah, we see the Lord reach in with his own arm (via the incarnation of his Son) to fix injustice, straighten what was bent, and provide salvation. The incarnation of Christ is the means God used to address the brokenness of his creation. Jesus is God's act of restorative justice.

THE WHOLE GOSPEL

Martin Luther, the great Protestant Reformer, often talked about this robust gospel that includes all the aspects of Jesus' life and ministry. The point of tension between the gospel, as Luther understood it, and Catholic theology centered on whether the forgiveness on the cross was to be earned or received. The result is that over time, many evangelicals created a shorthand version of the gospel that focuses on Jesus' death on the cross, the forgiveness of our sins, and the salvation of our souls. What we lose in the shorthand is the end to which the cross and forgiveness point and to which salvation is aimed.

Let's unpack a little bit of what is missed in the shorthand of the good news.

First, in 1 Corinthians 15, Paul tells us clearly that if Jesus didn't rise from the dead, then our faith is empty and worthless (1 Corinthians 15:19). If the cross was the sum total of the good news, it seems strange that Easter Sunday is the happiest day of the Christian calendar. Additionally, it was Jesus' human, sinless life that allowed the cross to accomplish its work—his righteousness for our unrighteousness. Therefore it seems that the story of the good news must include Jesus' birth and life as a sinless human. We can't take the cross out of our understanding of the good news and hold it up as a stand-alone event. The cross is necessarily bound up with the other aspects of the whole gospel: the story of God's act of restorative justice—his redemptive work in the birth, ministry, death, resurrection, ascension, and promised return of Jesus Christ.

Second, what we're talking about here is righteousness that isn't limited to purely spiritual matters but also includes justice. Jesus' engagement with fixing physical problems and addressing poverty not only speaks to what was lacking during the time of Isaiah but also fulfills Isaiah 58; 61, and other texts—prophecies of setting captives free, healing the lame, and giving sight to the blind. Jesus even used his fixing, or restoration, of what was broken as proof of his identity when the disciples of John the Baptist asked if he was the one to come. Like Aslan coming into Narnia, with winter melting away and the flowers of spring appearing underfoot, it is an inextricable part of the person, nature, and work of Jesus that the good news includes real change—both spiritually and materially.

When a pastor avows that it perverts the gospel to speak of justice instead of only the imputed righteousness of Jesus, I like to ask if I can repeat what I'm hearing in his argument to see if I understand correctly. I then reword his argument for effect and state:

> So Jesus came
> so that un*just* people
> could stand next to a *just* God
> as if we're *just*
> through a process of *just*ification
> whereby we're *just*ified.

The sarcasm is rarely missed.

Often a pastor who argues against the inclusion of justice in our understanding of the gospel has been using justice language all along without realizing it.

Third—and this one is shocking to most Christians—the cross is not the main point of our salvation. Put another way, the cross is a means, not an end. In Jerusalem, near where Jesus was crucified, stood the temple mount. The mount consisted of various parts: there were outer courts and, ultimately, the inner court, with an altar for sacrifices. Sacrifice, in Jewish theology, was the way to atone, or cleanse men and women of their sin so they could draw nearer to a holy God. Beyond the altar was the temple itself, which was a very high rectangular building broken into two parts. The first was the holy place, and in the back was the most holy place, or the holy of holies, which was separated from the rest of the temple by a large veil or curtain hung from the ceiling. God's Spirit and the ark of the covenant inhabited the holy of holies, and only the high priest was able to enter the holy of holies, once a year. No matter how many sacrifices were offered, humans still bore a taint of sin incompatible with the presence of God.

When Jesus died on the cross just outside the city walls, Scripture tells us he was a Lamb sent to be a sacrifice to take away the sins of the world. This is why in the Gospels we hear people say "Behold the Lamb of God." Jesus is pictured as a Lamb in the book of Revelation, and it is no accident that his death occurred during Passover. Jesus' death on the cross, more than symbolically, points to the Passover festival, celebrated each year to remember the means by which God saved the Jewish people from slavery in Egypt. Jesus' death on the cross was the final sacrifice. Just as God saved Israel from Egypt via the sacrifice of a lamb, so too he saves all people who are in bondage to sin, by the sacrifice of Jesus, the perfect Lamb.

THE END OF THE CROSS

When Jesus died, we're told, the heavens shook and lightning flashed. At the same time, something very interesting happened on the temple mount. Now, if the cross were the main point, or the end—not just the means—of the good news, then when Jesus died we should expect the temple to crack or be broken. As in *The Lion, the Witch and the Wardrobe*, when the table on which the lion Aslan was slain cracked, the altar would never again need to be used.

But this is not what happened.

When Jesus died, nothing at all happened to the altar, but the temple's four-inch-thick veil was ripped from top to bottom. The temple veil's ripping symbolized that the division between God and humankind had been removed. Jesus died for our sins as a means to the end of restoring our relationship with God. The good news includes, but is not limited to, the cross of Jesus. As I said at the beginning of this chapter, the problem with the gospel—it's hard to believe—is that we've made it too cross centered. We've centered it on the means (the cross) rather than centering it on the end (the ripped temple veil) and the reconciliation of God's people back to himself.

In short, Jesus, who came to work for restorative justice, had accomplished reconciliation between God and his creation. The apostle Paul describes this event by saying, "God was reconciling the world to himself in Christ," and, even more tellingly, he continues, "And he has committed to us the message of reconciliation" (2 Corinthians 5:18-19).

To understand the gospel correctly, we must see the cross as a means to the end of restored relationship with God. To take it in isolation is to miss the point it served. To put it another way, if we say the gospel centers on the cross, we overemphasize the forgiveness of sins while underemphasizing the relationship that forgiveness restores.

Once again, just as in Isaiah 59, we see righteousness, justice, and salvation all woven together into a unity and aiming at reconciliation—which is justice language!

If this is true, then we ought to be able to see this picture painted in other passages of Scripture, and I believe we do. Here is one example:

Listen to me, my people;
>   hear me, my nation:
>   Instruction will go out from me;
>   my justice will become a light to the nations.
> My righteousness draws near speedily,
>   my salvation is on the way,
>   and my arm will bring justice to the nations.
> The islands will look to me
>   and wait in hope for my arm. (Isaiah 51:4-5)

We have been brought back into relationship with God through the incarnation, life, ministry, death, and resurrection of Jesus Christ. We are now empowered, with the Holy Spirit, to go into the world as the body of Christ. We are continuing his incarnation, with a mandate to love others in his name and to be witnesses of his saving power.

Not only does salvation have a personal dimension, but it also has a covenantal or communal dimension, and our relationship with God is indivisible from the nature of our relationships in this world. As in Isaiah 58, which talks about true worship in relationship to justice for others, Matthew 25 tells us Jesus equates our relationships with others to our relationship with him. In particular, Jesus points to the vulnerable and oppressed, saying, "Whatever you did not do for one of the least of these, you did not do for me" (Matthew 25:45).

It is not that our works save us. We are saved by grace. What I'm suggesting is that our salvation, wrought by Christ, is an act of restorative justice, baptizing us as new members in his body, into a shared missional reality. The cross might be the effectual cause of our salvation, but it accomplishes reconciliation. It might be the crux of human history and the watershed moment in our conversion, but it is only one part of the current and flow of the whole of the gospel of Jesus Christ.

Focusing only on the cross without understanding reconciliation is like seeing only the wedding ceremony without understanding marriage—the very thing it inaugurates. The people of Jesus' day knew the Messiah came to bring peace on earth, but they didn't understand how. Today we often talk about the how (the cross of Christ) but lose sight of its purpose: establishing peace on earth through redemption, reconciliation, and restoration.

We don't earn our salvation by doing justice; rather, we who are made just through Christ *become* just as part of our nature. We are caught up in the arc of God's right arm reconciling the world to himself in Christ Jesus—addressing injustice and establishing righteousness by the forgiveness of sins and the calling to himself, and making new, a people of God joining him in his re-creative work.

The simple, radical, biblical idea is that you cannot separate God from love, Christ from love, or God's children from the call to love. The heart of God for his children, creation, and the restoration of things to how they were designed to be is an inextricable part of his character. The Bible says that God is love and that justice is the footstool of his throne and the scepter by which he rules. Thus, by nature, justice should pulse in the veins of those indwelt by God's Holy Spirit. Ignacio Ellacuría once said, "Always remember that there is no conversion to God if there is no conversion to the oppressed."[3]

THE MINISTRY OF RECONCILIATION

This salvation involves the teaching of Jesus as well as the incarnation of Jesus in us. It involves us telling people about Christ but also being the hands and feet of Christ manifesting his love to a broken and dying world. The two extreme views of salvation in liberal and conservative Christianity that have developed over the last one hundred years are both departures from historical Christianity, with some on the one end denying the power of his atonement and the reality of salvation, and some on the other end denying the transforming work and radical justice involving the King's heralding his kingdom and healing the wounds of the world—including injustices involving poverty, gender, tribalism, power dynamics, the sick, and the oppressed.

And our love of neighbor is no small matter when it comes to how we are to be saved. This is illustrated by the fact that Jesus' story of neighborly love, the parable of the good Samaritan, was an ethical story told in response to a question about how to be saved. The compartmentalization we do on paper with our religious parsing and formulas about Jesus evaporates in the face of the man himself. Jesus represents truth *and* justice, Savior *and* King. Love and salvation are part of the same fabric.

We are both gospel agents and gospel recipients. Those reconciled and agents of reconciliation.

We who have been reconciled to God cannot therefore ignore the ministry of reconciliation—the call to live into a new and unified relational thinking unmarred by colonial categories of race. Whatever our starting point, true north for Christians is the throne in heaven where all tongues, tribes, and nations worship in solidarity—as it ought to be.

SEVEN

THE SALVATION INDUSTRIAL COMPLEX

Visit those who are sick, or who are in trouble, especially those whom God has made needy by age, or by other sickness, as the feeble, the blind, and the lame who are in poverty. These you shall relieve with your goods after your power and after their need, for thus biddeth the Gospel.

JOHN WYCLIFFE

LIKE MANY CHILDREN steeped in evangelical culture, I grew up with the notion that to be saved we simply asked Jesus into our heart. This was the most central thought in my mind regarding Jesus and Christianity. A familiar sketch by Bill Bright, founder of Campus Crusade for Christ, showing the cross bridging a chasm—between humans on one side and God on the other—was the defining image for what transpires when we asked Jesus into our heart. We cross over from death to life with the cross of Jesus acting as the bridge. Although it's a striking image, and not altogether inaccurate, I later learned this is not the biblical picture.

In Genesis 28, Jacob has his well-known dream, where he sees a ladder connecting heaven and earth, with angels ascending and descending on it. This verse suggests how we should see our relationship with Christ. Yes, there is a stairway to heaven, but contrary to the popular spiritual, *we* are not climbing Jacob's ladder. The truth about Jacob's ladder is that Jacob never climbed it; it was the angels who ascended and descended. The ladder was the mediating link between heaven and earth.

When Jesus, who was certainly well aware of Jacob's dream, describes himself, early in the Gospel of John, he uses the same imagery. He tells Nathanael, "Very truly I tell you, you will see heaven open, and the angels of God ascending and descending on the Son of Man" (John 1:51). Jesus likens himself, and his ministry, to a bridge between heaven and earth much like Jacob's ladder—not a bridge we climb or cross over but something connecting, or linking, heaven and earth, God and humankind.

Jesus is how we come to God, not just how we cross the sin-gap to get over to God. Jesus stands between us and God at all times, making the Father known to us and interceding for our sins. This is why "asking Jesus into my heart" is such a slippery concept—using Jesus as a bridge to cross over is a much different proposition from actually being connected to or in Christ.

A MODERN HISTORY OF SALVATION

The Sinner's Prayer developed, more or less, from the work of American revivalist and theologian Charles Finney. Finney was a leader during the Second Great Awakening, which lasted from 1825 to 1835. During this time, Finney developed a methodology for converting people. He worked their emotions, often by juxtaposing hell and the offer of salvation, and he would call people to the "anxious seat," where they would talk with a representative, receive prayer, and, it was hoped, accept Christ for their salvation. This is the forerunner of what we know today as an altar call.

As Iain Murray argues in his seminal work *Revival and Revivalism*, Finney's innovation took revival from a Spirit-born response to the preaching of God's love—as revival was defined for decades, across multiple cities and denominations, prior to the Great Awakening—to a mechanical methodology that could be performed on any given night at any given revival meeting. The act of salvation went from something beyond our control to something we could plan for and lead.

When I used to drive from northern Virginia to South Carolina, where I attended college, I often passed small churches posting signs for an upcoming Friday-night revival. These signs, and their predicting when revival would come, clearly illustrate the change in revivalist thinking before and after Finney. Finney's lectures on revival were codified, put into book form, and made the basis for the development of revivalism in America. It was a movement that came to dominate frontier preaching as well as urban revival meetings featuring such hallmark names as Dwight Moody, Billy Sunday, and Billy Graham. The idea of revival is now so familiar to modern Christians we often mistakenly believe that "the Sinner's Prayer" and "asking Jesus into your heart" are phrases and ideas that have always existed.

The idea of asking Jesus into your heart primarily comes from two places in Scripture. First, Romans 10:9 says, "If you declare with your mouth, 'Jesus is Lord,' and believe in your heart that God raised him from the dead, you will be saved." Second, in the letter to the Laodiceans found in the book of Revelation, Jesus is depicted as saying, "Here I am! I stand at the door and knock. If anyone hears my voice and opens the door, I will come in and eat with that person, and they with me" (Revelation 3:20).

In the first instance, we misinterpret the verse when we lose sight of the Roman culture to which Paul was writing. The empire had a creedal formula of allegiance to the emperor, which basically stated that Caesar was lord. Paul counseled the readers of his letter that unless you confess with your lips and actually believe in your heart that Jesus, not Caesar, is the Lord—both the ruler and the definer of reality—you will not be identified with Jesus.

I once heard about a story from missionaries to Indonesia in which they asked a local pastor about some Christians they routinely saw at the school and mission compound. The pastor replied, "Oh, those aren't Christians." The missionaries were confused. The pastor continued,

"Well, they're Christians in here, but outside these walls they haven't identified with Christ. Until they do, they haven't truly confessed Christ." Although none of us truly know the state of a person's heart, this story does illustrate what Paul meant by confessing Jesus as Lord and believing in your heart. It's not meant to be an internalized or private affair done primarily with our eyes closed, but a reality we enter into with our eyes wide open.

Similarly, we often misunderstand the context of Jesus' knocking in Revelation 3. This is such a popular verse related to "salvation" that it is printed on hamburger wrappers of the West Coast's In-N-Out burger chain. The context in Revelation, however, clarifies that Jesus is knocking not at the door of an individual's heart but at the door of a community's gathering, and thereby indicating that their understanding of life and how they expressed themselves in the world was lacking Christ.

As often as we hear about accepting Jesus into our heart, this is not the usual salvation language found in the Bible. Scripture most often uses the image of our being *found in Christ*.[1] This was Paul's favorite idiom for the Christian life: "in Christ," or a related variant, is found over two hundred times in his writing. For example, 2 Corinthians 5:21 reads, "God made him who had no sin to be sin for us, so that *in him* we might become the righteousness of God." The union in Christ central to Paul's theology is the fulfillment of John 14:20, "On that day you will realize that I am in my Father, and you are in me, and I am in you."

Certainly our individual hearts are involved in our relationship with God, but the biblical language never alludes to Jesus in our hearts. Romans 5:5 tells us that "God's love has been poured out into our hearts through the Holy Spirit, who has been given to us." Galatians 4:6 similarly states that "God sent the Spirit of his Son into our hearts," and 2 Corinthians 1:22 notes that that God "put his Spirit in our hearts as a deposit, guaranteeing what is to come."

"Asking Jesus into your heart" carries the idea that we can have a personal relationship with Jesus. When evangelicalism was birthed during the First Great Awakening through revivals across England and America, the idea of a personal relationship stood in contrast to an impersonal, formulaic religious life associated with the Church of England. This newfound intimacy with God was, in part, the cause for the shift toward a greater focus on evangelism in that era and following.

I know from experience that we *can* have a personal relationship with Christ. The danger, however, comes when asking Jesus "into your heart" is reduced to merely a transaction of spiritual goods and rights. This is especially dangerous in a consumeristic society that places more emphasis on individual rights than on responsibilities. Many conservatives worry about what is known as the social gospel, but I wonder if we should be equally leery of the personal gospel on the other extreme.

Biblical texts on salvation and discipleship speak to both the personal and the social as part of an inextricable whole. If I follow Christ, it means I go where Christ goes. We follow him into the places where he leads. We don't just tuck "baby Jesus" into our heart and continue on with our own life and agendas.

G. K. Chesterton warned of the subtle danger of misappropriating the good news with only a personal view in mind in his 1909 book *What I Saw in America*: "The devil can quote Scripture for his purpose; and the text of Scripture which he now most commonly quotes is, 'The Kingdom of heaven is within you.' That text has been the stay and support of more Pharisees and prigs and self-righteous spiritual bullies than all the dogmas in creation; it has served to identify self-satisfaction with the peace that passes all understanding."

Chesterton continues by beautifully counseling:

> The text to be quoted in answer to it is that which declares that no man can receive the kingdom except as a little child. What we are to have inside is a childlike spirit; but the childlike spirit

is not entirely concerned about what is inside. It is the first mark of possessing it that one is interested in what is outside. The most childlike thing about a child is his curiosity and his appetite and his power of wonder at the world. *We might almost say that the whole advantage of having the kingdom within is that we look for it somewhere else.*[2]

The reduction of God's good news in Jesus to a magic formula—from relationship to transaction—allows a highly personalized and consumer approach to salvation. Instead of requiring everything, it requires nothing.

PEDDLING JESUS

When I worked at Christian camps for several summers, my fellow counselors and I couldn't help but notice the girl who came forward each summer in tears to receive Jesus. A few joked, "What? Did it not take last year?"

It is not a funny matter. It is profoundly sad.

With such an emphasis on converting people with a transactional formula, especially in the hands of young men and women who often lack formal theological or pastoral training, the race (dare I say competition?) to convert was always present.

As time went on, I began to realize the subtle economic forces undergirding the drive for conversions as well. The more "conversions" there were to report, the more success there was for camp directors to share with the camp's board of directors and major donors. And in the end, as is the case with success in most businesses, more conversions translated to more money.

At its best, this model of salvation was a beautiful way of introducing young people to the love of God in Jesus Christ; at its worst, it was a salvation industrial complex—a self-reinforcing system designed at propagating itself more than the reality it was created to serve.

I'm not completely against the Sinner's Prayer. In fact, my dad first met Jesus at a Billy Graham crusade back in 1958. What I am concerned with is the complete lack of biblical context that often is attached to modern revival teaching. Most revivalists would not say that the Christian life stops with the Sinner's Prayer, but without the appropriate context and teaching, it's easy to miss the rest of the story.

If the understanding of salvation we receive at the beginning is so truncated or disconnected from the whole story of Christ and the good news of restorative justice, it is no wonder that we have such a difficult time understanding how we bear any responsibility with regard to justice in society. Working for justice might seem like a *good* thing but not a *necessary* one.

Charles Finney believed a true conversion would result in a changed life, and he was an ardent abolitionist, delivering his abolitionist message in his sermons. Lisa Sharon Harper recounts that those who came forward at his revivals were directly pointed to sign up for the movement.[3] For him, coming to Christ was necessarily connected with standing against the oppression of brothers and sisters.

But truncated doctrines of salvation can explain a lot of radical ways in which Christians have compartmentalized faith throughout history to allow for such inconsistent thought and action as professing love of Jesus while committing gross injustice against our neighbor.

The Afrikaners in South Africa were highly religious and had developed a unique form of Calvinism that justified their conquest and exploitation of native Africans. They believed that they were the new Israel, God's elect, and that "black people were the descendants of Ham, the cursed. It would therefore be unthinkable that the 'blacks' could be considered the Afrikaner's equal."[4]

When Christ is "mine" rather than "ours," it is a lot easier to create the vertical hierarchies we have today. In Galatians 3:28 Paul writes, "There is neither Jew nor Gentile, neither slave nor free, nor is there male and female, for you are all one in Christ Jesus." In his book *From*

Every People and Nation, professor and theologian J. Daniel Hays writes in no uncertain terms: "Racial segregation among the people of God is a movement away from following God's redemptive plan."[5]

"Love your neighbor" shows up in sermons more easily than it does in relationship with the other.

Disconnected from "your will be done on earth as it is in heaven," our theology becomes permission to remain in our privilege, unengaged with the messier parts of reality.

Our own personal salvation, taken in isolation, as it has been done for much of history since revivalism, takes a page of the good news and makes it the whole story. Instead of "God so loved the world," we consume the gospel only as "God so loved me." We become merely recipients of grace and not agents of grace. Or, as Dietrich Bonhoeffer puts it in his famous work *The Cost of Discipleship*, we buy into a message of cheap grace rather than costly grace and hear "Come and live" without first hearing Christ bid us, "Come and die."

THE GOLDEN RULE (REMEMBERED)

Most all of us have heard of the golden rule: "Do to others as you would have them do to you" (Matthew 7:12; Luke 6:31). Sadly, this rule is all too often twisted into another that is only subtly different in structure but in fact can become a radical reinterpretation of the rule. Throughout history, it has been referred to as the "silver rule": "Do not do to others as you would not have them do to you."

The addition of the word *not* changes the emphasis completely. While the golden rule demands action—do to others—the silver rule allows for passivity: do not do to others. Just actions become optional. All too often we demonstrate a subtle preference for the silver rule by going only so far as to avoid intentionally wronging or harming others. The silver rule doesn't require us to intervene in injustice, as the golden rule does. Simply put, it may keep me from stealing, but it doesn't demand generosity. It may mean I don't tell racist jokes, but it doesn't demand that I pursue reconciliation.

The golden rule commands us to do good—to act. The silver rule asks us only not to do bad—to refrain from acting. The difference between the two is striking.

In antebellum America, slavery was a hotly contested subject. Some abolitionists gave action to their beliefs and donated what they could to the cause, even helping slaves escape to freedom. There were also those who believed slavery was wrong and did nothing. While the people who made up the latter group may have not been guilty of keeping slaves themselves, they took no action—beyond voicing opposition—to help end slavery. Here we see action versus passivity—gold versus silver.

The problem with the silver rule is that it matches so perfectly with the "do no harm" premise undergirding American ethical thinking. Put another way, we Americans tend to believe we can do anything we want as long as it doesn't hurt anyone else. Often, without realizing it, Christians live by the silver rule while feeling fully justified in their moral standing. Jesus and the golden rule didn't leave room for this. In fact, in Matthew 25, Jesus famously puts it like this: whatever you did for one of the least of these, you did for me, and whatever you *didn't do* for one of the least of these, you didn't do for me.

The pursuit of equality with our brother is a necessity. The rich or self-righteous can attack their brother as Cain attacked Abel, or, as in the parable of the good Samaritan, ignore him, but the truth remains that we are our brother's keeper.

BACK TO BONHOEFFER

Bonhoeffer is a recent example of someone standing against injustice through his solidarity with the Jews of Germany during World War II. What many don't know is that his evolution toward standing with the Jews in his country was significantly shaped by his time living in Harlem, New York, and interacting with the neighborhood's Abyssinian Baptist Church while studying at Union Theological Seminary in the 1930s.

Throughout this time he moved from a position as a wealthy, privileged theologian toward using his privilege on behalf of others. Because of this he chose to return to Germany just before the outbreak of war rather than to stay safe, but detached, in the United States.

As Reggie Williams notes in his seminal work *Bonhoeffer's Black Jesus*, "Bonhoeffer remains the only prominent white theologian of the twentieth century to speak about racism as a Christian problem. As a white man, Bonhoeffer had access to multiple audiences in opposition to racial discrimination that were not available to people of color, and he appropriated what he learned during his time in Harlem for that purpose."[6] He was there during the Harlem Renaissance, when the figure of the black Jesus emerged as a representation of the suffering Christian's solidarity with the suffering of African Americans. Williams wrote, "The demand for recognition by African Americans in the Harlem Renaissance was a demand for justice that can only come with the acknowledgment of their co-humanity, and Bonhoeffer's emphasis on being with and for others as a theological concept included a social and psychological dynamic of humanizing others and interrupting their abuse."[7]

Bonhoeffer understood that the gospel isn't a transaction but a radically redefining *relationship* necessarily affecting all the desires of the heart and all of life's relationships. His introduction to African American life helped him realize that this radical redefining and discipleship involved standing with others as Jesus did. In *The Cost of Discipleship*, Bonhoeffer zeroes in on our tendency to rationalize away the simple obedience required in following Jesus. Obedience, he says, is not a works-based formula for earning salvation but a necessary part of what it means to be in Christ.

He writes, "If Jesus said: leave everything else behind and follow me, leave your profession, your family, your people, and your father's house, then the biblical hearer knew that the only answer to this call is simple obedience, because the promise of community with Jesus is given to this obedience."[8] Though the hearer would understand this, Bonhoeffer says, we tend to explain away such a radical call by saying:

> Jesus' call is to be taken "absolutely seriously," but true obedience to it consists of my staying in my profession and in my family and serving him there, in true inner freedom. Thus, Jesus would call: come out!—but we would understand that he actually meant: stay in!—of course, as one who has inwardly come out. Or Jesus would say, do not worry; but we would understand: of course we should worry and work for our families and ourselves. Anything else would be irresponsible. But inwardly we should be free of such worry. . . . Everywhere it is the same—the deliberate avoidance of simple, literal obedience.[9]

A transactional understanding of salvation enables such rationalization and individualization. The way in which we understand coming to Jesus shapes and defines how we understand following Jesus.

What does a discussion of the Sinner's Prayer have to do with race and privilege?

Possibly everything.

EIGHT

A SHORT LOOK AT AMERICAN INDIVIDUALISM

We could search the world over, but we could not find a man
so low, so degraded, or so far below the social, economic,
and moral norms that we have established for ourselves
that he had not been created in the image of God.

CHARLES HODGE, THEOLOGIAN (1797-1898)

IN THE PREVIOUS CHAPTER, I discussed how the evangelical understanding of Jesus' salvation message moved from a Spirit-born response to something far less relational and very transactional. Why was this view so easy to integrate into the mainstream American church?

Americans have always had a deep commitment to individualism. From the Protestant work ethic, to the doctrine of self-reliance promulgated by Ralph Waldo Emerson and Henry David Thoreau, to the picture of the hardworking immigrant, we are shaped by stories of individual lives and the aspirations of great men and women. French historian Alexis de Tocqueville, as early as 1831 in his famous work *Democracy in America*, which details his experiences in America, makes repeated and powerful observations on the nature of American individualism:

I see an innumerable multitude of men, alike and equal, constantly circling around in pursuit of the petty and banal pleasures with which they glut their souls. Each of them withdrawn into himself, is almost unaware of the fate of the rest. Mankind, for him, consists in his children and his personal friends. As for the rest of his fellow citizens, they are near enough, but he does not notice them. He touches them but feels nothing. He exists in and for himself, and though he still may have a family, one can at least say that he has not got a fatherland.[1]

Tocqueville noted many admirable things about the United States—and he happened to see this particular flaw as well.

We are all complicit in American individualism. In fact, from childhood we are set up to be complicit. Individualism is a raw, overriding commitment to self-preservation and self-actualization. Radical individualism doesn't find a home in Christ's teaching and misses the theology of the body of Christ.

When God—existing eternally as three in one—created humankind, he said, "Let *us* create humankind in our image" (Genesis 1:26 NRSV).

I realized this only recently: the image of God is thoroughly communal. We cannot fully experience the image of a triune God when we are in isolation.

From Genesis 1 comes the basic, foundational premise for a theology of race: *all people are created in the image of God—together.* This gives every individual of every race in the world a remarkable status before God and in relation to humankind. It demolishes every theory of racial superiority or racial inferiority. As theologian Gary Deddo writes:

> Human identity cannot be grounded ultimately in race. The human being is essentially constituted by its relationship to God as the creature, reconciled sinner and glorified child of God. Who we are is determined in and through this relationship, and on the basis of this identity we are called to relate to others as those who also belong to God in this three-fold way.[2]

The Old Testament is replete with covenantal language between God, his creation, and his people, which demonstrates that, on many levels, our relationship with God is as a collective, or corporate, identity. Additionally, the New Testament letters use Greek terms of address meaning "you all" when speaking of the Christian community.

We are individuals. But we are made for and exist in community.

Faith is something we each own personally, but faith is also necessarily bound up in the matrix of God's covenant family and God's creation.

Sometimes I come upon truth as I ponder Scripture and experience on my own. But often truth is revealed to me by another with a more accurate perspective.

Martin Luther King Jr. spoke often of how human beings are all created equal in the eyes of God. In his sermon "The American Dream," delivered in July 1965 at Ebenezer Baptist Church, he said, "And we must never forget this as a nation: There are no gradations in the image of God. Every man from a treble white to a bass black is significant on God's keyboard, precisely because every man is made in the image of God. One day we will learn that. We will know one day that God made us to live together as brothers and to respect the dignity and worth of every man."[3]

God crowned humankind with his own glory. Tragically, we have turned the diversity of peoples into a hierarchy rather than a beautiful picture of people all made in the image of God, reconciled to God and to each other in Christ.

Soong-Chan Rah, author, theologian, and professor at North Park Theological Seminary, writes that if human beings are made in the image of God, then "racism declares, explicitly or implicitly, that the full expression of this image is found only in certain races. . . . The racialization of the *imago Dei* is a human attempt to elevate human standards above and in the place of God."[4] Psalm 8:4-5 says, "What is mankind that you are mindful of them, / human beings that you care for them? / You have made them a little lower than the angels / and crowned them with glory and honor." God made us out of dust but crowned us with his glory. Psalm 8 tells me that we should see the glory (the weightiness and value of God's image) before the dust (the messiness of our humanity). When we see people rightly, we see the crown of God's glory before the person. When we see them wrongly, we see the person before the crown—we see the dust before the glory.

HUMILITY AND GROWTH

As I gain a deeper understanding of race and culture, I don't agree with everything I read or hear. I often hesitate or disagree. However, I'm ever more aware that when I feel differently or disagree, I might be wrong. Truth is, as I learn from many of my friends, I'm often wrong.

It's tempting to think when we've learned a little bit of something that we've really *learned* it.

I remember my Greek professor telling the class after our first year that "a little bit of Greek is a dangerous thing." In other words, learning to read the easiest Greek texts in the Bible (for example, 1 John) can easily lead to overestimating one's knowledge or ability to read the rest.

Likewise, a little bit of insight into racial injustice or knowledge of America's racialized history can be a dangerous thing. I can't count how many times I've made the leap from learning a little bit or a little bit more about race to thinking I fully grasp the issue.

With an issue so complex we don't go from not knowing to knowing, as if a light switch were flipped on. Deeply complex and nuanced subjects take a lifetime of engagement and lead us down paths with lots of twists and turns, successes and mistakes.

Everyone wants to think they have a good understanding of race. We often treat it like a yes-or-no category. Are you racist? No. Therefore, are you good with race? Yes. The problem is, it's *not* a yes-or-no category but something with a hundred layers of nuance.

Are you a good swimmer?

Is your character good?

Are you a good citizen?

It would be easy to say yes to any of the above, but obviously, context matters. Am I a good swimmer compared to those on a swim team or to the kids in the neighborhood pool? Is my character good? I want to think so. But is it as it should be? Is it better now that I'm busy with four daughters and stressed about finances? Or am I making more compromises than I did a few years ago? Am I a good citizen? Well, certainly. But compared to whom?

Often the thing you believe you are good at is the thing you're not working on getting any better at. And often the thing you're not working at getting better at is the thing you're not good at.

As a white man writing a book on privilege, I've had to admit from the beginning that my understanding and knowledge of racism end when conversation turns to the firsthand experiences of people of color.

Many of these first-person experiences of racism have roots in the complex web of subconscious racial bias we—whether white or people of color—carry with us. The way that modern racism hides in the shadows of our minds is what we'll turn to next.

PART III

THE CHALLENGE OF PRIVILEGE

NINE

WHEN RACISM WENT UNDERGROUND

Implicit Racial Bias and the Stories That Hide Within Us

> Of all the liars in the world, sometimes the worst are our own fears.
>
> **RUDYARD KIPLING**

> Lying to ourselves is more deeply ingrained than lying to others.
>
> **FYODOR DOSTOYEVSKY**

I BECAME A CHRISTIAN at the age of twenty-two, while I was attending Clemson University, and I began attending a church with new Christian friends. One friend whose family lived forty-five minutes away had a father who was a Baptist preacher. One Sunday, we all drove to his church to hear him preach. Afterward we joined my friend's family for Sunday dinner at their house.

At the dinner table, the preacher and I started discussing history after he learned of my love for the subject. Somehow the conversation turned to the Civil War, a subject that has long fascinated me. He leaned forward and began to speak emphatically.

"Do you know the war wasn't even about slavery?" he asked. "It was about states' rights."

I responded rather quickly and directly with a pointed question of my own, "States' rights about *what*?" Of course on the surface the Civil War was about states' rights (and there are plenty of historians who will argue this), but I was rather shocked and amused at what I considered a ludicrous deflecting of *what* the southern states had disagreed with the North about and *why* they chose to secede from the Union soon after Lincoln was elected president. I underscored my point by adding, "You cannot remove slavery from an honest conversation on the Civil War."

He didn't back down. "I can defend slavery from the Bible," he said.

I was surprised at the direction he was going. I responded, "The kind of chattel slavery that was practiced in the antebellum South?"

He quickly became frustrated with me, and the conversation ended. In fact, for the remainder of the day, as everyone watched NFL football, he largely ignored me and I him.

This experience opened my eyes to the fact that racism can exist even within church walls. It also showed me that by lessening the gravity of the injustices of the past, we somehow attempt to lessen any blame for those injustices. The lesser the crime, the lesser the punishment. The closer it is to some category in biblical times, the more excusable it is. What most disturbed me was that as this pastor played word games with history, he was willfully denying something about the nature of justice and desecrating the idea of biblical love—that we must do for others what we would have them do for us. What's more, he was an evangelist for his compartmentalized thinking. He propagated a kind of racial thinking that I can only assume was passed on to him by prior generations and which he was passing along, as well.

Through this experience and many others, my perspective on overt racism within society changed drastically during those college years in South Carolina. It's not that everyone living in the South is viciously racist. But I confronted racism in new ways there. I learned about the significant influence of generational and cultural thinking about race. To break such cycles, we parents must make intentional choices about what we will communicate to our children—and what biases from our own childhood we will *not* pass on.

Many times our racial posture is acquired based on our being raised in a certain place, at a given time, with particular cultural perspectives. How we are socialized shapes our inner self more than we realize. To mature, however, means to be willing to subject our views to biblical and historical scrutiny.

And this brings me back to the chaplain early in this book who wasn't allowed to let a speaker use the phrase *white privilege*. Our desire for truth has to outweigh our commitment to comfort or reinforcing cultural biases.

IMPLICIT MEMORIES

Discussing controversial topics is complicated by our common assumption that we know more than we actually do. Without knowing it, we have likely been on one side of the fence because of our social circles, or we unconciously choose news programs that will reinforce our ideas. Like politics, abortion, or welfare, race is a topic that engenders passion. As a result, when we try to talk about race we often become defensive, and effective communication is cut short.

When the topic of race comes up in conversation, many insist that there is no longer racism in America. After all, segregation is illegal, and we have prominent leaders of color in all dimensions of society. We even had a black president. Yet most of us understand that racial divides persist in our country. Only 7 percent of Americans think racism is just a problem of the past.[1] We can't point to signs of overt institutional racism such as "whites only" bathrooms, but we are aware that strains of racism linger. Turning on the news any evening makes it clear.

When we're defensive in conversations about race, we lose the opportunity to learn and more fully understand the issue. And one thing we badly need to understand is the implicit, subconscious nature of racism. *Implicit* means people are not making an intentional choice to be racist. Nonetheless, undernearth our conscious awareness, race shapes and affects our decisions and actions.

When I was in graduate school, I did an independent study with a psychology professor, Todd Hall. One of the fascinating topics we examined, and an important area of research for him, was implicit memories. By definition, implicit memories are different from the explicit memories we can call to mind—I remember what chocolate ice cream tastes like, I remember collecting baseball cards as a teenager, I remember going to Yosemite with my dad in 1999. I'm consciously aware of, and reflect on, explicit memories.

Implicit memories are stored in your brain and body, but they exist beneath your level of conscious remembrance. They include shortcuts your brain creates over time so it doesn't have to reflect on each new piece of data in order to decide how to handle it. Or they stem from a trauma or other powerful experiences that create a physical manifestation, such that an experience similar to the past trauma results in the same physical response. My professor gave me an example: a college student walks to the front door of the library with his backpack full of books, forgetting that one of them hasn't been checked out— and sets off the security alarm. A month later, the same student leaves the library with no backpack and no books. As he walks toward the library exit, suddenly his heart begins to race, his body temperature goes up, and his shoulders tighten up—all manifestations of fear. The earlier experience created an implicit memory, and even if the student knows he is not stealing books, his body chemistry now has a "button" that is triggered by the library's security gate.

Such shortcuts are often created early in life, and we have no conscious memory of the original experiences. We have buttons—if we hear or see something that connects to a significant memory or experience, it hits the button. Sometimes something as simple as a sight, a sound, or a smell will push one of those buttons. Nevertheless, we usually are only vaguely aware of the cause and effect or how the pattern came to exist in us in the first place.

Even if we haven't learned about implicit memories through academic study, we all understand what they are in a practical sense. When a person's emotional response (output) seems inconsistent with what's going on (the input), it's often because an implicit memory has been triggered. Implicit memories can play a powerful role in shaping our responses to situations or in how we physically react under certain circumstances. Because of this, implicit memories are involved in the ways we understand people.

HOW WE SEE COLOR

Awareness of implicit memories can help us understand how race becomes socialized, programmed, or baked into our subconscious in ways that shape our thinking and behavior, whether we're consciously aware of it or not. One of the shortcuts many Americans have made in the last several decades is connected to "government handouts." In radio interviews and public events I've come across a lot of people who fall into the trap of thinking about people of color when they initially think of poverty. It's not a natural connection based on empirical data; rather, it's a result of the way poverty has been represented. It's one of the more fascinating examples because it's a socially constructed implicit memory based on pictures (and rhetoric) that we have seen connected to poverty in our lifetime—an image that shifted drastically over the course of the 1900s.

In a class at Kilns College, I used the following example to demonstrate how society creates many social constructs for us. Before 1964—especially during the Depression era—the common image of poverty was of white rural men, women, and children. Often they were Dust Bowl migrants and the like. But now, when many in society think of poor people, they primarily picture African Americans standing in lines at homeless shelters or rescue missions, or hanging out in the ghettos.

This despite the fact that during the Depression era and beyond, there have been large populations of poor black people (this is one reason why Martin Luther King Jr. made poverty the focus of his work near the end of his life), and likewise of poor whites who were homeless and surviving on food stamps. Though the percentages of those in poverty by race differ significantly, the overall numbers of poor whites and poor blacks in the United States are quite comparable. Yet we have certain pictures of what poverty looks like, based on how poverty is portrayed in the media and elsewhere, not on the actual statistics.

One of my graduate students, a creative pastor in Detroit, came across a Yale project that cataloged 170,000 photographs of the Depression era and made them searchable online. After hearing my lecture, he began digging into the database to explore what I had mentioned in class. When he searched the photos using the tags "negro," "negroes," "black," and "African," only about 2,200 photos came up, or roughly 1 percent of the photos. When he searched "poor," there were 153 photos with that tag, and only a few pictured minorities.[2] Following up on his email, I searched "poor" and the results were overwhelmingly of rural life, in contrast to our predominantly urban view of poverty today. When I searched "poor" with "negro," only two of the 153 "poor"-tagged photos featured African Americans. The database provocatively illustrates how our racial views of poverty have shifted over time.

IMPLICIT RACIAL BIAS

As I said previously, implicit memories are one way race gets socialized into our subconscious so as to shape our thinking and behavior, whether we're aware of it or not. This leads us to a more recent field of study called implicit bias.

Implicit bias is the missing part of the conversation among people who don't think they are racist and who don't want to be racist. We still find ourselves caught in a tangled web where race shapes our thoughts and actions. Even among well-meaning, supposedly post-racial people, somehow race ends up playing a significant factor in the outcomes of events and experiences.

Implicit bias is a relatively new area of study that first came onto the scene in the 1990s and has since garnered significant research across a wide array of issues. The phrase refers to "the attitudes or stereotypes affecting our understanding, actions, and decisions in an unconscious manner."[3] People respond both positively and negatively—and such responses are involuntary, occurring without our awareness or intention.[4] Implicit biases include not only the implicit memories we have but also the shortcuts our brains have made in determining what things should elicit a fight response or a flight response. If a person is socialized to connect fear with brown or black bodies, then they will have a strong implicit racial bias (reaction) when they see a brown or black body in an unfamiliar setting.

I watched this happen once on a United flight leaving Chicago. An older white woman sitting next to a window tensed up when a thirty-year-old black man walked down the aisle—even before he took the middle seat between her and me. Throughout the three-hour flight, the good-natured African American man tried to make conversation with her, but she kept her body defensively angled toward the window. This woman might say she's not racist, meaning she doesn't think she's racist, but her implicit racial bias was unmistakable.

Implicit biases have been measured to test how they relate to gender, body weight, religion, sexuality, and race, and they have been assessed in many fields including criminal justice, housing, health care, employment, and education.[5] The findings include these: biases occur among those who profess to be impartial, such as judges; they do not necessarily correspond with our professed beliefs and views; and they generally favor our own group and affect our actual behavior.[6]

For example, a recent study of job interviews for low-wage jobs revealed that when even all interviewees had equivalent experience on their résumés, whites were twice as likely to be called back. Even if the white applicant was said to have just been released from prison, the black applicants still received fewer callbacks. Similarly, in a study where identical résumés—some with stereotypically black names— were sent to potential employers, a "white" name increased the likelihood of being called back by 50 percent. In a completely different realm, when researchers offered iPods for sale online, 21 percent more offers were made for the iPods held by a white hand versus photos depicting the iPods being held by a black hand.[7]

Consider the issue from another angle. Social psychologist Claude M. Steele's book *Whistling Vivaldi* includes the story of Brent Staples, a young man of color who realized that he could assuage the implicit fears of white people by whistling melody lines from Vivaldi—in other words, he could reduce implicit racial bias by exhibiting white culture.[8]

Earlier I discussed the doll experiment that Thurgood Marshall cited in *Brown v. Board of Education*. More recently, a similar study was covered in the documentary *A Girl like Me* and revealed—in ways that would grieve any parent—that although we are now together in many respects, we are still not equal. The video shows young black girls selecting which dolls looked bad or good, pretty or ugly. When asked, they select the black doll as looking "bad," and when they are asked why, they say, "Because she's black."[9] Watching a video of young people demonstrating internalized oppression and self-hatred, resulting from racial bias in society, is heartbreaking.

I often encounter people who tell me that we may not have equality of outcome in America, but there is definitely equality of opportunity. I used to believe this, but it's not true.

Implicit racism in the United States today leads to the same results as the explicit racism of the Jim Crow era. Those who experience it are not treated equally and consequently do not enjoy the same opportunities.

When racial bias is implicit, it is easy to overlook, so we assume that we're free of racism. It is also complicated because implicit racial bias shows up among people of color, not just in the majority culture, and it affects the ways they perceive themselves and others. In short, this bias is much more subtle and hidden than explicit racism.

To whatever degree implicit racial bias is present, it is dangerous. For Christians who are working for a society of the equality amid diversity that is God's dream for the world, implicit bias is the battleground where we need to fight the hardest.

TRAYVON, TAMIR, AND GRAND JURIES

Implicit racial bias is also one of the reasons we find people on such radically opposing sides when it comes to a grand jury's decisions on evidence for an indictment in the shooting of unarmed persons of color. On one side we find people crying for justice, and on the other we find people who can't understand why a grand jury failure to indict doesn't constitute justice.

The 2014 shooting of Tamir Rice is a good example of the compounding effects of implicit bias. The event involved many layers, a bit like the game of telephone most of us played as children. It started with a 911 call reporting a guy with a pistol who kept taking it in and out of his pants and pointing it at people. Several times the caller said the gun was "probably fake" and later that the person with the gun was "probably a juvenile."[10] The 911 operator didn't enter all of the information provided by the caller into the police system. Subsequently, the police dispatcher did not give that information to the police. The police were told there was a black male with a gun and they should respond "code three"—the highest priority, demanding immediate response.[11] By the time the police arrived, they were relying on their own implicit shortcuts—and they shot twelve-year-old Tamir within two seconds.

Here's the point: no one got up that morning determined to kill a young black boy. However, as circumstances played themselves out and information moved from one person to the next, implicit racial bias increased the possibility, and then led to the sad actuality, of the shooting of a young boy who was holding a toy gun. Implicit bias, like a computing error, can be compounded from one iteration to the next in a chain of events.

After such a tragedy, many of the men and women on a grand jury readily empathize with the shooter (police officer or otherwise), sensing that if they were put in the same situation, they might have done the same thing. It logically follows that if I might have done the same thing, then the shooting must have been justified. At this point, finding the evidence surrounding the shooter's actions sufficient for an indictment becomes very difficult. The end result is that everyone except for the grieving mother—and the child lying dead in the park—receives sympathy.

If we return to our game of telephone, does saying "black" at the beginning of the chain of details provided make it more dangerous for a person than if they had been white? A study revealed that when participants were shown a picture of a man, followed by a picture of either a tool or a weapon, they were more likely to misidentify tools as guns when the preceding picture was of an African American. On the flip side, they were more likely to misidentify a gun as a tool when the preceding picture showed a white man. Researcher Keith Payne comments, "In these experiments, people knew the correct response, but when they had to make snap judgments they were sometimes swayed by unconscious bias." He continues, "When they had enough time, they could almost always report correctly whether they were seeing a gun or a tool."[12]

When Trayvon Martin was shot by George Zimmerman in February 2012, another aspect of implicit bias affected how people viewed the event. The incident was a single story with two different people at its center. One was a Latino American, Zimmerman, patrolling neighborhood streets in an effort to fight crime. The other was a young African American teen staying with his father—who was visiting his fiancée—who lived in the same neighborhood as Zimmerman. One was the aggressor, while the other was minding his own business. By the time the shots were fired—with no eyewitnesses—the story had gotten complicated: the initial aggressor stated later that in the course of the struggle, he had become afraid for his life—and thus he was justified in "standing his ground" and shooting Martin.

We have one story, and there are two sets of shoes you can put yourself in. Did you see the events through George Zimmerman's eyes or Trayvon Martin's eyes? As someone pointed out to me, and as was confirmed in multiple conversations, many white evangelicals— without realizing it—identified with Zimmerman. Somehow, even though Zimmerman is Latino (his mother was born in Peru and had African-Latin ancestry through her grandmother), for many white evangelicals he was a more natural center of gravity than Trayvon was. The media infused this tragedy with their own biases by determining how to portray Trayvon. Was he a black man in a hoodie or a smiling seventeen-year-old student?

Meanwhile, most African Americans I know and spoke with immediately related to the racial profiling, and the horror of Zimmerman's vigilante actions, as Trayvon might have experienced it.

Why was it more comfortable—with one story and two narratives— for so many to land in George Zimmerman's shoes? Could the answer be that a deep implicit racial bias was at work?

Often, it seems, we are less concerned with equality and justice than we are subconsciously guided by our instincts toward comfort, safety, and security. That means it becomes possible for us to have conversations about justice, believing we're fully invested in ethical principles, while actually guarding our own threatened self as a higher priority. When the conversation forces us to choose one side or another, the bias comes to light.

We need to recognize that implicit racial bias can be so powerful it can prompt us to take someone's life, and it can compound and multiply throughout a group so as to collectively justify the hasty taking of a life made in God's image.

Grand juries weigh whether there is sufficient evidence to send a case to trial. The trial is where all the evidence is heard, where it becomes a matter of public record, where everyone can observe the process, and where a unanimous verdict must be reached. Those who clamor for justice after unarmed shootings are not declaring the shooter guilty and demanding a sentence. Rather, they are demanding that over time in an open environment, the process go far enough that any implicit bias at work can be exposed and addressed. They simply desire that the system work well enough to allow us to confidently declare that in the end, whether there's a sentence or not, justice has been done. This doesn't mean every police shooting should go to an open trial or that every grand jury is wrong; it simply means we need to acknowledge the role implicit racial bias can play in a closed-room hearing that doesn't require a unanimous conclusion. And we need to ensure that the law is actually blind—remember the classical statue of blindfolded Lady Justice holding balanced scales?

MICHELANGELO AND OUR GREAT WHITE GOD

Because how we view things in our minds plays such a powerful role in shaping how we see the world, we need to focus on the accuracy of our picture of the history of our faith.

An interesting way of contemplating this is to ask, *Is God white?*

Of course he's not. Isn't that a silly question? God is a Spirit and, although a person in the fullest sense, he is not human.

When I ask, "Is God white?" I'm betting that most people in our culture experience a quick (possibly even unconscious) mental flash of Michelangelo's famous portrait of God as a fiery older European male imparting his Spirit into Adam's reclining body, one of the central scenes in the ceiling frescoes of the Sistine Chapel.

The Sistine Chapel was restored under Pope Sixtus IV in the late 1400s. Pope Sixtus IV is regarded as one of the most corrupt and licentious of the Renaissance popes; he was also guilty of a lot of nepotism—

gifting religious offices and titles to family members. One of the cardinals he appointed was his nephew Della Roverae. This nephew in turn became Pope Julius, known to history as the warrior pope. Julius commissioned Michelangelo to adorn the ceiling of the Sistine Chapel as a way of honoring his uncle and their family.

Until the Renaissance, the image of God the Father was rarely painted in either Eastern or Western Christendom. Churches in various traditions had regularly depicted Jesus in mosaics and paintings and would sometimes represent the Holy Spirit as a dove, or the Holy Spirit and the Father as symbols, but rarely was God seen in human form.

Michelangelo's image of God was painted white in 1512. What Michelangelo did was groundbreaking.

So what color was Jesus?

When most Americans think of Jews, they likely tend to picture the European Jews most Americans have seen in countless clips from World War II and the Holocaust. The Jewish people in Europe were descendants of the Diaspora (or scattering), which came about after countless conquests of Israel/Judah and the eventual destruction of the temple in Jerusalem by the Romans.

Palestine—the name the Romans gave to the thin strip of land between Egypt below and the east-west trade routes of Asia Minor—remained a populated space long after the Diaspora. Jews and Christians lived there. Following the Muslim conquests, the area was continuously inhabited by Jewish, Christian, and Muslim Palestinians until the modern era.

In all likelihood, Jesus was browner than the thousands of paintings that have come down to us in the Western tradition, and browner than the hundreds of movie portrayals of him.

If we take Jesus' words literally when he says, "If you see me you have seen the Father," then we should be inclined to portray God (if we do at all) as closer to a Palestinian than a white European.

Why was Jesus played by Ewan McGregor in a 2015 movie? Why was Moses played by Christian Bale? I think it's because we in the majority culture like our biblical heroes to look like our superheroes—to look like us.

These images perpetuate a form of white normalcy, or standard, without our even realizing it.

In *The Christian Imagination*, Willie Jennings delineates how Christian theology and growth was constructed around whiteness in the European Christianity of the 1500s. Black skin was used to indicate "doubt" and "uncertainty" about salvation, while white skin was seen as "rooted in the signs of movement toward God."[13] In other words, whiteness was seen as more closely resembling God and thus increased the likelihood of salvation.

CONCLUSION

People are quick to disavow any shred of personal racism, yet subconscious racism is embedded in us and has tangible effects in our communities. Are we still responsible even for racism that we're not conscious of? The Old Testament's Levitical law deals with sins of ignorance: a transgression is a transgression whether it is intentional or not, and regardless of our awareness of it. Our justice system today upholds a similar principle: *ignorantia juris non excusat*, or "ignorance of the law excuses no one."

Think about how you feel when someone causes you serious harm. Rarely would their assurances of good intentions make you feel any better or resolve the situation.

Instead of putting energy into denying that we're racist, a more transparent and honest response might be to admit our desire to be free from racist thinking—and commit ourselves to searching for latent forms of bias within ourselves and trying to address them.

The good news is that research shows our implicit biases can be overcome. The study about the tools and guns showed that when people were given more time, they were able to correctly identify the item regardless of the race of the man in the prior image. A study by economists found that NBA referees were more likely to call fouls on players of another race, and likewise white baseball umpires were less likely to expand the strike zone for black pitchers. But several years later the economists repeated the study on the NBA referees and found that the bias had disappeared. This suggested that when we understand our bias, we can adjust our behavior and act more fairly.[14] Overall research indicates that we are able to reduce or eliminate implicit bias through counterstereotypic training and exposure, education and awareness about bias, having contact with people outside our in-group, and examining and incorporating other viewpoints.[15]

Even the words we use matter. Christena Cleveland writes that simply using the terms *us* and *them* causes us to prefer ourselves and things associated with us, and those we consider like us, over others. The same research shows when we simply begin to use more inclusive language, we begin to repair the divide: "If we begin to use inclusive language such as *we* and *us* (rather than *they* and *them*) when we refer to the different groups in the body of Christ, we will begin to associate the different groups with the same positive attributes and feelings that we associate with ourselves."[16]

TEN

THE VOICE OF JUSTICE

> Truth, like gold, is to be obtained not by its growth,
> but by washing away from it all that is not gold.

LEO TOLSTOY

LIBERATION THEOLOGY, one of the distinctive theological expressions of the twentieth century, emerged from the Latin American experience of systemic injustice and poverty. First articulated by Gustavo Gutiérrez in his 1971 book *A Theology of Liberation* and modeled in the lives and teachings of other Catholic priests such as Oscar Romero and Leonardo Boff, it has developed into an international movement. This doctrine is notable for its focus on God's preferential treatment of the poor and oppressed, a confrontation with empires and worldly powers, and an unyielding commitment to the realization of a different kind of kingdom that ultimately puts social justice squarely at the forefront.

I remember first hearing about liberation theology—almost always in a negative light. It was criticized for being a dangerous system that could lead to an erroneous interpretation of Scripture from a socialist perspective. I've come to learn that most of these warnings came from people who hadn't actually studied it. If they did study it, they must have missed the strong justice calling in Scripture, which I've spent the last decade attempting to highlight.

Again, our spheres of influence reinforce normative behaviors and belief and also teach us which divergent streams of thought are threatening or dangerous to our way of life.

I now find that there is much in liberation theology that can be—
and needs to be—heard as a corrective to our individualized approach
to Scripture, as well as calling out the blinders we often have when
reading the Bible, which filter out the emphasis on the poor while
selecting texts to allow them to craft a gospel of comfort for those who
(by the world's standards) are rich.

Liberation theology has exposed the power dynamics that exploit
the poor and oppressed, and it highlights the dignity of the oppressed and the necessity of hearing their voices. Renowned South
American educator Paolo Freire's *Pedagogy of the Oppressed* echoes
such themes.

Have you ever heard the phrase *voice for the voiceless?* Most of us
have used it at some point—certainly I have on numerous occasions.
It sounds good and noble, but we should pause before saying it. People
are not voiceless. Everyone has a voice, and we don't need to speak for
them. Instead we need to understand and address the processes that
steal their voices or the reasons we aren't hearing them.

RICHARD TWISS AND DIVERSITY
AT CHRISTIAN CONFERENCES

One of the more important people and voices in my life over the last
decade was my friend the late Richard Twiss.[1] Richard, a descendant
of the Lakota Sioux of South Dakota, was a scholar, writer, speaker,
thought leader, and follower of Jesus.

Richard was one of the most personable and charismatic individuals I've ever met. I've never known someone so authentic and full
of love as to make everyone with whom he spent time feel so special
and valuable. Richard was also one of the sharpest prophetic voices
I've ever heard. He was unyielding with regard to logic and truth. He
was hard as nails when it came to excuses from those who would argue
with truth or try to compromise truth out of fear.

Truth, for Richard, was unwavering.

If I were able to ask Richard today how best to honor him, I know that after talking about his concern for his wife, kids, and grandkids, he would expect me to use my voice to speak truth. In fact, I think it would confuse Richard if I, or any of his other friends, failed to give voice to his arguments, his call, and his critique of modern American Christian culture on behalf of indigenous people and other people groups who have been marginalized and oppressed.

Richard helped open my eyes and shape my thinking regarding the problem of power structures and the differences in opportunity within the evangelical world. White males are on one end of the power spectrum, while minorities and women have historically been on the other.

This shows up prominently in the lack of diversity on the roster of teachers and presenters at Christian conferences and events. Simply open up any recent Christian magazine and look at the full-page conference ads. It won't take long before the lack of diversity in speakers becomes apparent.

It can be hard for organizers to include other voices in planning. It requires stepping outside their comfortable circle of friends (who often look and think a lot like they do) and finding a diversity of voices who can speak on issues of theology, justice, leadership, and other topics.

Speaker diversity was never an issue I felt responsible to champion, however. Although I have cared about this issue and wanted to support my friends, I always felt like my "lack of ethnicity" made this a topic to which I couldn't authentically speak.

I don't feel that way anymore.

I have begun to realize this is my issue to champion, not simply in support of my friends or because it is valid, but also *because I am a white man*. I'm realizing there needs to be a plurality of voices calling for diversity. They should not be limited to the voices of experts but should also include the voices of those who are learning and being challenged as they go. Acknowledging truth, Richard might say, brings with it the ethical imperative to join its chorus.

In the final analysis, the lack of diversity in conference planning and the neglect of diverse representation within the typical speaker lineup at Christian conferences is a justice issue. Without diversity we fail to challenge long-held notions. Equally destructive, we continue to reaffirm and reinforce the stereotype that only those with white faces are smart enough, creative enough, and powerful enough to teach, lead, and inspire the body of Christ.

Failing to make ethnic and gender diversity a priority is a subtle way of creating or perpetuating a form of class distinction. If our first instinct is to keep doing what is familiar, which leaves many of the real experts in this topic unheard, people of color and women, by implication, come off as inferior or "less than." Lack of diversity hurts and affects everyone.

Perpetuating a system we inherit is the same as creating the system anew for those who come after us. To pass along is to create. We are either building a diverse representation of leaders for a diverse church or facilitating a poor and unjust representation of a dominant-culture church.

Richard Twiss taught me a lot in this regard. He pointed out that after four hundred years of mission work with Native American communities, most evangelicals neither can name a single Native leader nor have ever seen or heard a Native speaker at a national-level conference. This, by any and all standards, would seem like a failure of leadership development and empowerment.

Many white male evangelicals may agree with these arguments but prefer not to live them out in practice. It means an increase in competition for speaking engagements and leadership opportunities, giving up some of one's personal platform so that others may rise. Often the first reaction among white speakers is that it feels unfair. But it is a good thing to see more nonwhite speakers and leaders. The truth is that the increase in competition for white males and difficulty of being heard will only feel the way it has always felt for most women and male leaders of color until now.

The point is not to be down on white men, but to be up on equality. It's not that white men with something to say are bad or that all conference organizers get it wrong. But as both a white man and a former conference organizer, I'm learning the need to actively seek diverse representation in decision making, leadership, and speaker scheduling. To the degree we do not, we are consciously or unconsciously discriminating and thereby doing a disservice to the kingdom.

To be clear, diversity doesn't trump competency, character, or having a message. Leaders and teachers have—and should have—a high bar of accountability with regard to teaching and influence. We need to be aware, however, that implicit racial bias might shape our understanding of others or how we appreciate, or not, the expertise of others.

Further, we need to operate with the theologically confident belief that when we create the opportunity, God can and will bring credible, diverse, and dynamic voices. As he does, they will lead us into a fuller, more equitable, and more representative picture of the body of Christ.

I'm not an expert on race. My academic background isn't in diversity or reconciliation, but in philosophy and religion. I am growing and being challenged in these areas myself. However, I can—just as much as anyone else—use my voice for what is right and just.

DIVERSITY . . .

Toward this end, one of the things I have realized and begun to teach is that the message is not only in the content of *what* is taught or presented but also in *who* is bringing it. Indeed, when we address injustices and fight for the oppressed, we can fall into suppressing those we seek to liberate by failing either to shift the power dynamic or to recognize the need for promoting the first-person voice of the oppressed.

We saw this happen in the late 1800s during the social gospel movement, when issues of race began to be a focus of ministers with a heart for justice. In *The Cross and the Lynching Tree* James Cone tells us how the "Social Gospel advocates held conferences on the status of the Negro in Mohonk, New York, in 1890 and 1891 and felt no need to invite any blacks, because, as Lyman Abbott said, 'A patient is not invited to the consultation of the doctors on his case.'"[2]

You may think that was then and this is now, that we have moved beyond such paternalism. But the representation or voice often still remains absent in key places of power focused on justice, including nonprofit leadership, and therefore nonprofit funding.

Currently, only 14 percent of foundation board members are non-white, and only 6 percent of foundation board presidents are non-white.[3] Simple math shows that 94 percent of foundation boards are white. However a great amount of sociological research indicates the importance of diversity in organizations and decision making. Christena Cleveland, associate professor of the practice of reconciliation at Duke University, writes that "leadership teams that make decisions in a homogenous vacuum are more likely to make less informed decisions while perceiving that their decision is superior to those of other groups"—practicing what has come to be known as *groupthink*.[4] Conversely, more diverse teams are better able to produce effective and creative solutions to challenges because they benefit from a broader array of knowledge, ideas, resources, and experience.

The lack of diversity in nonprofit leadership also means that white middle-class organizations are more likely to get funding, because they fit the cultural norms and expectations of the donating foundations. Because there are so few voices of color on the boards, different perspectives in decision making that could encourage more diversity in funding are missing. In fact, nonwhite-run nonprofits receive only 3 percent of funding.[5]

White-led organizations serving people of color can also be problematic. Such leaders cannot fully understand the people, values, and cultures of those they are serving. The neighborhoods in which they have projects often have leaders who have been living and serving there for a long time, yet they are often overlooked in favor of white middle-class missionary types. I've heard several minority pastor friends lament a new urban church plant moving into their neighborhood with literature that claims the area is unchurched. The sad implication is that these multiethnic pastors either are considered not relevant or are being completely ignored by the white pastors and planting organizations moving into their neighborhoods.

My friend Leroy Barber is the cofounder and director of The Voices Project, an organization dedicated to shaping and influencing culture through training, promoting, and supporting leaders of color. Leroy consults with organizations serious about gathering diversity in their leadership and throughout their organizations and is the director of @HopeMob, which is dedicated to raising funds for organizations of color serving people of color. He has been living and serving in urban neighborhoods for over twenty-five years and has experienced funding inequality and the impact of well-meaning predominantly white Christians coming in to work with poor people of color.

In his book *Red, Brown, Yellow, Black, White—Who's More Precious in God's Sight?* Leroy writes about the phenomenon he has experienced many times: "Rather than fund Christians already living and working in the community to be served, white evangelicals favor funding urban missions like field trips for those outside the community. Money is given to support the field trippers rather than those who serve long-term in such urban missions."[6] He continues, "These invaders begin to represent and speak on behalf of the poor in the neighborhood. They are asked to sit in places of power, serve on boards, to speak, and to write. They may now begin to admire neighborhood champions and even open themselves up to learn from them, but they don't yield the opportunity to sit in places of power to those neighborhood champions."[7]

Boards and leadership circles often remain as they are unintentionally. We choose board members from our group of friends and acquaintances with whom we are comfortable. But if our circle of friends is not diverse, our leadership circles will not be either. If we want to reflect the redemptive mission of God in our lives and organizations, we need to be intentional about seeking diversity in our organizations and in our boards.

There are other places that inadvertently propagate a narrow stream of voices. Take Christian publishing—an arena that has long been noticeably white. Publishers, like any for-profit business, work with a business model that requires a certain number of products (in this case books) to be sold in order to keep the organization sustainable. There are boards and leaders whose jobs are to ensure this financial viability.

Editors and publishers who acquire authors know what type of person will sell books and what demographic purchases the most books. For a long time, signing a pastor of a suburban church with a substantial budget and a large number of wealthy members who are educated and well connected proved to be a successful model. Suburban churches often put large sums of money into outreach and outside ministries that create connections to others outside their community and even internationally. For a pastor of such a church who has authored a book, this often results in increased sales.

Contrast this with a minority pastor who works in an inner-city context with a small, less-educated congregation. It's possible that this urban pastor is doing more community development, working to find deep and practical ways to contextualize theology for people in need.

It doesn't take long to see how some of the best voices with depth and nitty-gritty experience don't fit the economic models of the publishing industry. There are many publishers—such as InterVarsity Press—intentionally trying to shift this power dynamic, but the fact remains that for a long time Christian publishing has mirrored back to us the same lack of diversity with which our own lives and congregations are challenged. After all, consumers shape the business world as much as the business world shapes consumers.

Archbishop Oscar Romero, who was viciously gunned down in March 1980 in El Salvador for speaking truth to power, famously said, "It is not enough to undertake works of charity to alleviate the suffering of the poor; we must transform the structures that create this suffering."

THE PROBLEM WITH CHARITY AND COMPASSION *FOR* OTHERS

Back in 2010, when we began The Justice Conference, evangelicalism was in a great space with regard to increased global awareness. Bono had for several years called Americans to awareness of the reality of HIV/ AIDS in Africa and the benefit of wearing "(RED)." The global epidemic of human slavery and sex trafficking stemming from the increased ease of travel—which is itself a result of globalization—was beginning to impress itself on the American psyche. Additionally, Americans, long complicit in tragedies such as the ongoing conflicts and exploitative diamond and mineral mines in places such as the Democratic Republic of Congo, were beginning to open their eyes to the nature of consumerism and its effects on the poor and oppressed half a world away.

The surge in awareness of injustice was matched by a wave of compassion. Many joined causes aiming to end some of the world's great evils. I myself was calling people to many of these causes and leading people into many of these places.

Slowly we began to realize—and I continue to see this as I travel—the subtle ways in which compassion, although a good thing, often gets in the way of our pursuit of justice. There are at least three ways I've seen this happen.

First, it can lead to a mistaken belief that compassion *is* justice, rather than a *component* of deep, rich, and more holistic justice. Doing acts of compassion is different from helping to make sure people exist in a just state. Those who seek to provide help to others must search out the underlying causes for observable needs. If we don't, we may provide resources to meet what we see as the need while actually causing harm to those we are trying to help. If causes are embraced without education, creating relationships, and finding a balance of power, white privilege can run rampant.

An excess of privilege plus a surplus of guilt equals an outflow of compassion. Compassion ministries sometimes pacify the giver's guilt without remedying the injustice suffered by the poor. Compassion is certainly a start, but it needs to be informed, or it may stop short of providing authentic justice.

Further, short-term missions may reinforce the very American idea that we can be anything and do anything—simply because of our wealth and privilege, not because we have worked to develop relationships with the people we aim to help, nor because we have any real long-term commitment or expertise in providing solutions for the needs.

The goal here is to develop reciprocity and mutuality, where we learn from and are being led by those we are serving, not just giving them something we have.

Second, compassion ministries can lead us to believe that justice is simply a cause. So we begin to think that if we have a cause we're doing justice. But the biblical call isn't just to have a cause or to pursue justice in a certain arena, but to *become* just. Putting all of our energy into a cause can lead to burnout rather than a life dedicated to growing more just, as followers of Christ, in every way that we live and move and have our being.

Last, compassion as our only form of justice feeds our hero or savior complexes. Compassion can often be self-serving, meeting our needs for adventure and building our social media persona.

Posting pictures with African children while on a short-term mission trip is a much more complicated act than many of us initially understand. While such images may seem cute and innocent, sharing them may reinforce a power differential; we begin to look like a savior, set apart, a white face smiling in the midst of a throng of black faces in need. We regularly see these pictures, don't we? Of course the motive and heart of the person involved isn't to harm others, but think how curious it is that we don't often do the same thing at home: seek out groups of kids in the children's ministry at church or in the neighborhood and pose for group pictures with them. The fact that we take pictures of ourselves with groups of African children abroad, but not groups of white children at home, points to the subtle way our understanding of compassion can actually be about elevating ourselves at the expense of the people we serve.

Charity gives, but love serves. True justice is costly.

Distilled down to simple terms, privilege and guilt often result in attempts at offering compassion to those we deem to have needs. Compassion does not equal justice. Justice does not equate to participation in some cause or another.

NORMALIZE OUR EXPERIENCE

Rather than practice compassion at a distance or as a project, we must look below the surface. What systemic injustices do we continue to perpetuate, and how can we change course? How do we intentionally make way for other voices? The need for diversity is a theological and sociological issue.

From a Christian point of view, it is our responsibility to take an active role in fostering views of reality that are theologically true and are generous pictures of others, free from racial bias.

In my book *Create vs. Copy* I wrote about the importance of making space for life in our pursuit of justice. My friend Wynand de Kock was instrumental in helping me realize this. Based on Genesis 1:1-10, he believes God's primary creative act was to separate light and dark and the heavens and the earth—all before bringing life into being. In other words, God's first impulse of creativity, like an artist's preparing of a canvas, was to make space for life. Real, physical space.

De Kock writes, "When I think about God and what He is passionate about, one of the first things that comes to my mind is that He makes space for people to know His life-giving presence. God makes space for life—space in which we can engage him."[8] We see this in the exodus, when God leads his people into the Promised Land. Psalm 23 bears witness to the the space—the table—God provides and maintains for us: "You prepare a table for me / in the presence of my enemies." It is also expressed when Jesus talks of tearing down the temple and rebuilding it in three days. The temple was the place where people were able to meet with God. It was a space created for relationship. Jesus' prophecy about tearing down the literal temple and replacing it with himself is a strong allusion to the relational space he was creating for us to be with God. Space for life is a necessity if we're to practice peace and goodness.

As we grow in our understanding of justice, we embrace and create space for diverse voices. Miroslav Volf, celebrated theologian and professor at Yale Divinity School, writes, "When God sets out to embrace the enemy, the result is the cross. . . . Having been embraced by God, we must make space for others in ourselves and invite them in—even our enemies. This is what we enact as we celebrate the Eucharist. In receiving Christ's broken body and spilled blood, in a sense, we receive all those whom Christ received by suffering."[9]

If the throne of heaven is the center for diversity and worship in the book of Revelation, then the Eucharist or Communion table, where we recognize the body and blood of Christ, should be the center for diversity in the age of the church. We cannot fully participate in the body of Christ as a divided people.

Jesus himself knew this. He counseled those who would come to the altar to drop their sacrifice in order to go and be reconciled with their brother or sister first. Unity with the other is necessary for experiencing full oneness with God. The theme of unity dominates Jesus' last conversation with the Father before the cross. In John 17, Jesus earnestly prays that we would be one as he and the Father are one. Again, this oneness is a necessary component to full understanding and experience of God. Our American individualism benefits us when we rely on ourselves, but it fails when we cannot see our lives as bound up with the lives of others.

Theologically, our division—or lack of unity in diversity—is not accidental, minor, or of secondary concern. God cannot fully be known until we find ways to be one with each other and to come as one united church to the Lord's Supper.

Only in Christ do we see that the call to full unity in our beautiful and God-given diversity is necessary and central to our individual and collective program of being found with and in God. And this move toward unity, as underscored by the picture of the cross and the symbols of Communion, necessarily calls forth sacrifice. How can unity be achieved if the individual parts are not willing to compromise on their particular desires—their sense of autonomy or human will— in order to find the fullness of community required for our greatest human flourishing and experience of God?

The problem of race and soft segregation in America should not be seen as awkward, challenging, or easy to dismiss because it is too difficult to address. Rather, by facing the mess and challenge of race, we are pursuing a path whereby we can better understand our own humanity and more fully experience the diversity and oneness of the divine Trinity.

We can invite people into our spaces and to our tables.

Soft segregation ends through hard commitments. And that work isn't easy.

Ending soft segregation requires commitment. It requires more than including different voices; it also requires redistributing the power differentials and opportunity. My friends Leroy Barber and David Bailey talk about being able to be among a group of white folks as peers, but knowing they are present only because they are among the best in their fields—while the whites around them are sometimes just mediocre in theirs. David breaks it down this way: "White privilege allows you to be average and sit in places of power because of relationship. Relationships that were formed because of de facto segregation in cities, schools, churches."

To change that system, we whites have to give away our power and steward our privilege. While research tells us diversity has a positive impact on groups and communities, it also points to possible negative consequences if *all* members of a group do not have equal status or feel valued by their peers. Cleveland writes, "If issues of status, privilege and power are not effectively addressed within the cross-cultural situation, existing divisions will deepen and widen."[10]

Our lack of diversity is the result of a segregated social structure that started hundreds of years ago. Unless we actively try to reform it, vestiges of it will continue to wreak harm for a long time to come. It is only by slowly and methodically making diversity an organizational priority that it will change.

The church is certainly not the only arena that has suffered from a lack of diversity. It is heartening to see other efforts to change this. For example, several years ago leaders of the National Football League realized that although a majority of its players were African American, only 6 percent of coaches were. In 2003 it instituted the Rooney Rule—named for Dan Rooney, the leader of the diversity committee—to ensure minorities were considered for high-level coaching positions. By 2007 the percentage of African American coaches had jumped to 22 percent.[11]

There is a power to our own decisions, and we need to take seriously the ability to create change.

ELEVEN

FINDING OURSELVES IN THE OTHER

If we have no peace, it is because we have
forgotten that we belong to each other.

MOTHER TERESA

I believe in the Holy Spirit, the holy catholic church,
the communion of saints, the forgiveness of sins, the
resurrection of the body, and the life everlasting. Amen.

THE APOSTLES' CREED

AT THE HEART OF THE ISSUE of race is identity. White identity, for most of us, is the freedom from ever having to face obstacles because of the color of our skin. Nonwhite identity is—in the modern era—the difficulty of being defined as being different from the white standard. Even in this paragraph I'm demonstrating the problem: I didn't say black and nonblack; I said white and nonwhite, the two categories our racialized culture allows for. And I'd be willing to guess that you didn't even notice it.

WHEN YOUR CREATION MYTH CRUMBLES

I was at a church in Atlanta in a gathering for students of Historically Black Colleges and Universities (HBCUs) when a young man asked a question about identity and history. His question surfaced in a unique way the reality that the creation myth, or sense of beginning, undergirding black identity in America is rooted in a very different place from mine—that of a white American.

Much of our identity is derived from our past, our cultural heritage— where we've come from. For black children in America, their story often begins with slavery. That is a radically different foundation on which to build your identity than the foundation on which most white people have built theirs. The white American "creation story," as it was framed in the melting-pot analogy of the 1940s and '50s, is positive and exciting: a country forged in the "untamed wilderness" out of nothing more than healthy doses of curiosity and courage and a thirst for liberty, freedom, and—ironically—equality.

The black American creation story, Asian American creation story, Latin American creation story, and Native American creation story are rooted in tragedy, kidnapping, enslavement, theft, coercion, rape, murder, genocide, inequality, exclusion, terrorism, and oppression in this country, all because of the color of their ancestors' skin. There is no denying the powerful psychological influence of such a heritage, nor the difficulty involved with forging an identity out of such a painful past.

What does it do to someone when their identity is always "up from" slavery? What challenge does it present to a young man or woman's sense of dignity when they are forced to spend their energy escaping identification with a deeply historical category and struggling to demonstrate their individual worth?

On that same trip, one of my pastor friends from Chicago was selling sweatshirts that said "King me" and "Queen me." The sweatshirts were a reference to the kings and queens of Africa—the nobility—from whom African Americans are descended.

At the conference, Rudy Rasmus, an over-sixty pastor who is well-known for his work in Houston over recent decades (as well as for being Beyoncé's pastor), fielded a question about the #BlackLivesMatter campaign. Rasmus grew up in segregated Houston as a child, and when asked about #BlackLivesMatter, his response was "It's about time." And then he gently continued, "I wish someone would have told me as a little kid, 'Your little black life matters.'"

I have known my whole life that my life mattered. I can't imagine the pain and hopelessness that Rudy was referring to. On another occasion, Rudy told his audience how as a child he loved to go to the zoo. His reason wasn't to see the animals but because it was the only place where there was only *one* water fountain—a fountain coming out of the head of a lion—where all children drank together. Growing up under Jim Crow, Rudy loved the zoo because it gave him the ability to feel equal.

The story we're told as children powerfully influences our sense of identity and hope. As a white son of an immigrant, I identified readily with the nobler aspects of American history. I was told that being born American was the best thing that could happen to a person, and I owned every bit of that heritage. Hopefully, after reading this book, you and I can agree that being born American might not always have been the best thing for many people.

I have Asian American friends who get asked at children's sports games when they immigrated based on the sound of their first or last name—despite being third- or fourth-generation Americans. Ironically, though I'm only a second-generation American, I have always been "obviously" American, and no one asks me those questions. The lack of normative Anglo and Christian names leads people to mistakenly assume that these Asian American families are "the other," different or new.

A COSTLY DREAM

Our idealized white standard of success is tinged with aspects of the American dream, the Protestant work ethic, the spirit of entrepreneurship, a latent form of pride, and the need to feel superior to what we see in other countries. With our hyperinflated sense of American individualism and lack of communal awareness, the standard becomes a challenge for minorities who are outside it, and even many white people find themselves failing to meet the the standard, lacking the language to articulate the reason.

Nobel Prize–winning economist Joseph Stiglitz, well-known for his analysis of inequality in America, writes, "Horatio Alger–style rags-to-riches stories were not a deliberate hoax, but given how they've lulled us into a sense of complacency, they might as well have been." He continues, "The upwardly mobile American is becoming a statistical oddity. . . . Only fifty-eight percent of Americans born into the bottom fifth of income earners move out of that category, and just six percent born into the bottom fifth move into the top. Economic mobility is lower in the United States than in most of Europe and lower than in all of Scandinavia."[1] Regardless of the color of our skin, very few of us are achieving our expected level of prosperity, and that causes frustration, angst, and alienation.

Often white people caught *beneath* the white standard dismiss those caught *outside* the white standard because they don't feel like they have benefited in any way from being white, but there is a real difference between those historically caught under and those caught outside the system. On top of their inability to live the American dream, minorities in America have experienced terrorism (lynching and other violence), discrimination in the form of policies and policing, and a relentless, ongoing sense of being kept outside mainstream culture.

Identity can be a powerful force for empowering or oppressing, uniting or dividing. Jesus deconstructed the set of teachings he received about identity. Are we willing to have our received set of teachings about identity deconstructed?

COMMUNION OF SAINTS

Stanley Hauerwas, theologian, ethicist, and professor at Duke University, states, "The church is constituted as a new people who have been gathered from the nations to remind the world that we are in fact one people. Gathering, therefore, is an eschatological act as it is the foretaste of the unity of the communion of the saints."[2]

The challenge of faith, just as when Peter walked on water, is to take our eyes off ourselves and our circumstances in order to walk by faith.

Faith looks outside itself.

Fear looks to itself.

As we participate with Jesus as part of one body, we are a gathering with no Jew or Gentile, slave or free, male or female. Not only are we destined for oneness, but in finding oneness we enjoy full participation in the image of God. Multicultural and diverse expressions are important not to fulfill a political or sociological agenda and demonstrate that we're free of racism—or even better, that we have genuine affection for everyone beyond our own groups. Rather, it is a theological imperative that the trajectory of our journey home to God and reconciliation with him is bound up in our reconciliation with others in the one body of Christ and united with our Creator God.

If we truly believe that our Christian journey involves following Christ into the broken parts of the world and seeking reconciliation with him, ourselves, our neighbor, and the rest of creation, we cannot ignore the brokenness in American race relations. And if we believe we are called to do more than passively wait for Jesus to return and transform the world in an instant, we should feel like we are compelled—even required—to act.

The list below is a way to begin moving down the road of laying down privilege and seeking responsible engagement in the lives of brothers and sisters of color. It is by no means perfect or holistic, but it's a great start for trying to engage the American history of racism and do something about it.

1. LISTEN AND LEARN

Depending on your background, the word *protest* may be a positive or a negative word. In my context, protesters and protesting are often associated with counterculturalism, antigovernment sentiment, violence, agitation, and anarchy. It's not uncommon where I live to hear someone say something like "If those people went and found jobs, they wouldn't have time to protest, and they wouldn't have anything to protest about."

But that's a caricature of protest. How would the Civil Rights Act have ever generated the momentum it did without the courageous men and women who participated in sit-ins, marches, and rallies? There is such a thing as righteous anger, and it is just.

Unfortunately, the establishment often finds ways to marginalize voices that create tension or anxiety. "Get a job," "stop being divisive," and "quit trying to cause trouble" are all ways of silencing voices that may have something urgent and important to say.

We need to learn again how to listen. How to hear. How to care enough about truth that we take information in rather than just broadcasting it out. Without broadening our circles, we will remain narrow.

We tend to assume we can reshuffle the puzzle pieces that are already on the table and construct better ways of thinking and being. Often, however, such construction requires adding information, depth, and other voices to the information we already have. It is a lack of faith, and a narrow view of the depth and richness of the body of Christ, that fears there will be no trustworthy, biblically faithful, or well-motivated people who might disagree with me or who I can learn from.

Listening isn't just about the content but also about whose voice carries it. There is a texture to truth that comes from those who have experienced something directly. As grateful as I am that you have read my book, it certainly isn't the first book ever written about this subject. There are countless books written by members of minorities with firsthand experience of American inequality that you *must* read if you want to understand the story of racism in America.

I've compiled a list of recommended reading from a number of different Christian thinkers and leaders, which is located at the end of this book. Look at the descriptions and Amazon reviews, and try reading some from a different perspective or that you might even disagree with. If we listen only to the voices that make us feel comfortable or that we already agree with, how can we ever grow or learn? Learning takes wrestling. True prayer and growth in wisdom are often born of confusion and dissonance—two things that make us most open to hearing from God.

Read books. Watch a documentary. Pursue a college or advanced degree. Listen to a different news channel.

Learn how to listen.

2. LAMENT

Walter Brueggemann in his book *Journey to the Common Good* writes, "Sabbath, in the first instance, is not about worship. It is about work stoppage. It is about withdrawal from the anxiety system of Pharaoh, the refusal to let one's life be defined by production and consumption and the endless pursuit of private well-being."[3]

As I mentioned earlier in the book, I struggle as both a teacher and a pastor. I care deeply about transmitting truth, but I struggle with being a people pleaser. Are we willing to follow Christ into the weeds, where people won't respond positively? Are we willing to own the fact that it is only because of our privilege that we are able to entertain that question?

Lament is an oft-neglected facet of the biblical narrative and experience in today's culture. As Soong-Chan Rah notes, "The Scriptures testify to the importance of lament. Nearly forty percent of the Psalms are laments. A quick glance through the Christian Copyright License International's list reveals that less than ten percent of those songs would even remotely qualify as laments. Our worship does not match the biblical testimony."[4] Scripture calls us to lament injustice. Not to rush in. Not to brush past. And not to excuse injustice as simply being the responsibility or fault of some other generation.

I often have a hard time preaching on Easter. My church knows this. More importantly, my wife knows this. She reminds me every year not to make the mistake of redoing the judgmental sermon of several Easters ago when something got under my saddle and I railed against the American Easter bunny, Easter baskets, pastel clothing, and nice dinners at the mother-in-law's house tradition we have built up around Jesus' resurrection rather than the radical, world-upending truth it is.

Despite regretting the judgmental tone of that Easter sermon, I meant every word I said in it. It infuriates me when we take stories like Easter—stories that stand against the way of the world—and tame them. We take a narrative that is all about killing the self and turn it into a consumer holiday.

This year I had the same angst when Easter morning rolled around. When my friend Pete asked me what I wanted to talk about, I said, "Race in America."

Talking about race plunges us closer to the faith required to follow Christ more than Easter baskets, doesn't it? It isn't a happy or exciting topic, but it certainly seems to be directly correlated with the story of Christ breaking into the world and our responsibility to continue his work. It also seems like it might lead to a lot more good in practice than excesses of chocolate for kids.

How can we have Easter without Good Friday, resurrection without the cross, celebration without lament?

When one part of the body of Christ suffers, the whole part suffers. How can we not share in the experience or narrative of others in the body of Christ?

Keeping our focus on ourselves is what allows us to reduce the work of God to self-help or consumable spiritual goods that can fill me or give me a spiritual experience when at the same moment, across national, racial, or socioeconomic divides, stands my brother or sister in suffering and lament.

Maybe Oscar Romero said it best: "There are many things that can only be seen through eyes that have cried."

3. CONFESSION

Several friends of mine, Mae Cannon, Lisa Sharon Harper, Troy Jackson, and Soong-Chan Rah, collaborated in 2014 to write a book titled *Forgive Us: Confessions of a Compromised Faith.* The book gives historical depth to various facets of the Christian church's complicity in injustice over time—or, more specifically, our corporate sins as the church of Jesus. It calls us to own and confess the complicated history of the church. Daniel 9 contains a long prayer in which Daniel confesses Israel's sins and asks forgiveness for them, even though he would have been too young to be guilty of committing them himself. Like Daniel, we must learn the corporate discipline of acknowledging the darker parts of church history and practice.

John Dawson writes,

> The greatest wounds in human history, the greatest injustices, have not happened through the acts of some individual perpetrator, but rather through the institutions, systems, philosophies, cultures, religions, and governments of mankind. Because of this, we, as individuals, are tempted to absolve ourselves of all individual responsibility. . . . Unless somebody identifies themselves with corporate entities, such as the nation of our citizenship or the subculture of our ancestors, the act of honest confession will never take place. This leaves us in a world of injury and offense in which no corporate sin is ever acknowledged, reconciliation never begins and old hatreds deepen.[5]

One of the pitfalls facing us is our American competitiveness: "You're not as good at diversity as I am," or "Your church doesn't have as many minorities as mine," or "I've walked at more rallies or posted more about racism on social media than you." If we allow that to happen, we're sunk.

Suddenly the work of restoration will twist back into being about us and our own achievement, rather than being about others and equality.

Instead of seeking to win, we must seek to collaborate. Instead of judging each other, we must learn how to encourage each other.

Are we aware of each other's creation narratives—whether good or bad? Are we aware of the damaging parts hidden in our own creation narrative or sense of cultural identity? Are we willing to be humble when we recognize that we don't?

This may be one of the most difficult things I have had to learn. I've started a church, nonprofit organizations, and a conference, all aimed at the common good. This can make it easy to fall into the delusion that the problems are because of "those" people, certainly not me. I'm the guy who's trying to make things right—what is it I would need to confess? The truth, however, is far more complex. I don't get everything right, and much of the good I do has resulted from systems of privilege where I have been the beneficiary.

Confession is the honest acceptance that in changing the world, we must not neglect the changes that need occur in us. And confession is the humble offering to the "other" that enables them to see we are not trying to fix them but are willing to take responsibility for, and join them in, the brokenness under which they suffer. Confession knits us together as brothers and sisters.

4. LAY DOWN PRIVILEGE

In a conversation with Soong-Chan Rah, he pointed out something I know to be true. He said, "If I say, 'All white folks should have a friend of color,' everyone would be okay with it. If I say, 'We need to dismantle white privilege,' everyone will castigate it."[6] White privilege is something we cannot ignore, and we must confront it.

Challenging people to compassion works. Challenging complicated structural issues, however, causes dissension and anxiety. But as we saw much earlier in the book, the prophetic voice is always at odds with the status quo, the powerful, and the privileged.

We don't lay down power or privilege easily, but repentance includes dismantling. That often means giving up something that is rightfully ours. Laying down privilege will look different for everyone, but here are some examples of different things I've done, or am doing, to challenge my privilege and to allow those outside the dominant culture to speak into my life.

So that the audience could hear from one of the voices I listen to, I yielded half of my time at The Justice Conference in Los Angeles in 2014 to a reputable Latina friend who brought a powerful message on unity.[7] Giving up positions of power and passing along opportunity to others is one of the most challenging—yet redemptive—lessons I've been trying to learn.

A colleague of mine and I are actively helping leaders of color from urban contexts (some who don't have the resources to be considered by traditional publishers) get published under a publishing label, Voices. Rather than expand and broaden our own voice, we are actively and creatively making space for other voices.

I raise money not just for the organizations I lead but for organizations that promote the encouragement and development of leaders of color who often have a difficult time securing funding.

Because I live in a state that is not very diverse, we prioritize bringing diversity in to our church through guest speakers, and we open our facility and host retreats to leaders of color.

It has been fun and liberating to engage in endeavors designed to benefit diversity rather than extend my privilege or advantage. Giving up patterns of privilege is difficult, but it is also rewarding. I can't take the credit for it, but our vacation calendar is now tied to that of several amazing friends—all leaders of color—that Tamara and I wouldn't miss spending time with for the world. Spending long nights under summer skies sharing drinks and conversation has produced some of the most humanizing and transformational experiences of our lives.

The list above includes things I've done or tried to do that might be helpful. They are not meant to be things I should be rewarded for. I'm a pilgrim on the journey of dismantling privilege. One of the greatest struggles is how to understand all the biblical language of fullness of life and joy while balancing these with responsibility to our neighbor. There is always more I can do, and there is more I can and will learn how to do. I am trying to submit to the Holy Spirit, and friends I trust, to let the Lord work on me.

I won't attempt to unpack these big ideas here, but two current political movements that are pointed at restoration and the dismantling of white privilege are affirmative action and reparations. If you feel stirred to learn more about privilege and the practical steps people are taking to try to address it, I recommend studying these two movements, regardless of what you already think about them.

One of the best examples of a need for recompense—and a lack thereof—involves the Belgian Congo. In case you aren't familiar with this piece of history, I'll summarize it briefly. In 1865 Leopold II became king of Belgium, and he quickly set out to build his empire. A primary focus for Leopold was acquiring a colony in Africa. In 1878 he hired famous explorer Henry Morton Stanley to launch extensive explorations of the Congo and to begin building bases and roads. Stanley was able to convince 450 leaders in the region to sign over their land to Leopold's International African Association. While this organization was ostensibly founded to bring progress, instead it systematically exploited the Congolese people. It is estimated that from 1880 to 1920 around ten million people, half of the population of the Congo Basin, died.[8] During his reign over the Congo Free State, Leopold managed to convince most of the world of his great "philanthropy," and he won awards for his humanitarian efforts. However, what was actually happening was deeply sinister—and he not only was fully aware of the extermination but also endorsed it.

In all, King Leopold amassed at least 220 million francs, an equivalent of $1.1 billion in today's dollars.[9] Upon his death, it took fourteen years to untangle Leopold's finances. He had hidden his wealth in various foundations, in secret companies, and with certain individuals in order to keep it from going to others. Belgian politicians and others filed lawsuits to stake their claim on his assets; and after official meetings and deliberations, the Belgian government eventually received most of the money. Historian Adam Hochschild provocatively states, "There was no lawyer to argue that the money should have been returned to the Congolese."[10]

America's situation is different from that of the Congo, or from South Africa for that matter, but it's curious to me how stark the lack of recompense is when I look outward toward other countries and how often I've been inclined to ignore or argue against it when we look inside, at our own.

Exodus 12:35-36 tells us that the Israelites, upon leaving their Egyptian slavery, "asked the Egyptians for jewelry of silver and gold, and for clothing, and the Lord had given the people favor in the sight of the Egyptians, so that they let them have what they asked. And so they plundered the Egyptians." Although I heard the story of the Israelites making a golden calf out of melted gold any number of times when I was growing up, I never thought about how the former slaves even had the gold to melt.

Many times "forty acres and a mule" is cited as a compensation supposedly received by formerly enslaved African descendants in the United States. But that is inaccurate; forty acres and a mule was never an official government policy. Rather, this was a field order (Special Field Order 15) issued by General William T. Sherman at the end of his march through the South in the Civil War. It was his attempt to give the freed slaves who had followed behind his army somewhere to go and a way to provide for themselves so he didn't have to. Ironically, then, the best example of restitution after American slavery didn't even come from the federal government but from one man's command in the field.

Another example of the unresolved lack of reparations emerges when we realized how most prominent politicians seeking the highest offices in our government never bother to campaign on Native American reservations. To honestly or effectively campaign before a group of people means you need to tell them of something that you either have done or are going to do to address the challenges, needs, and aspirations of their community. The failure by most politicians and their parties to publicly acknowledge the historic injustices against Native Americans or establish programs to address systemic issues in Native American communities means there is really no reason to go talk to them. If you don't have anything to say, it's easier to avoid the situation altogether. I had never really paid attention to, or thought about, whether presidential candidates campaign on reservations. I'm not sure many Americans do. I was shocked to learn that reservations have been completely absent from candidates' travel schedules in spite of the fact that Native Americans are willing to, are able to, and do vote in elections.

Reparations, in its fullest sense, doesn't mean we simply throw money at problems but that we seek to redress past injustices in order to reach a position of equality and equal opportunity. We have a long way to go as a nation in this regard.

By dismantling privilege, we are attempting to answer the biblical call to community. If we don't answer that call, we're missing something in our ecclesiology. And if we get defensive when something or someone challenges our view of community, our defensiveness shows that our ecclesiology is broken or infected by individualism.

It is only through the power and grace of the Holy Spirit that we can overcome half a millennium of cultural aggressions, racist policies, and abuse. It won't be easy. It won't happen quickly. It will be painful, arduous, and costly. We will make mistakes, we will hurt each other, and we will suffer setbacks along the way, but as we lay down our privilege and accept responsibility for the world in which we live, love of neighbor and true equality may yet shine through in our future.

THE REAL AMERICAN DREAM

One of my favorite history books is *The Real American Dream* by historian Andrew Delbanco. In this short and insightful book Delbanco argues that America's centering point, its focus of social cohesion, has involved three distinct movements.

The first movement was our identity under God. Whether Christian, deist, or other, early American society had a general collective identity as being created by and formed under the watchful eye of a Creator or the Almighty.

The second movement was our identity as a nation. It came in the years following the Civil War as Darwin's *On the Origin of Species* began to circulate, bringing a new, evolutionary worldview. This challenge to God, along with world events and the rise of imperialism, led to a galvanizing unity as Americans, with nation and country serving as our identity and centering principle. As Walt Whitman penned, "The United States themselves are essentially the greatest poem."[11]

This movement was especially strong following World War II, when dominant-culture Americans forged a shared identity through the trials of war.[12] The Greatest Generation, as it came to be known, was intensely patriotic, deeply proud, and respectful of the sacrifices so many had made in the global fight for freedom. Many still assumed or chose a Christian identity, but increasingly national identity emerged as a unifying social value.

The final movement emphasized identity as individuals. The hippie generation, influenced by the Beatnik poets, existential philosophy, and growing pluralistic forms of religion such as Zen Buddhism combined with disillusionment in "the establishment," strongly emphasized the individual and individual experience. With the subsequent loss of trust in the highest offices of the land through the Watergate trials and the complicated feelings surrounding the war in Vietnam, the third movement emerged. This most recent transition was away from national pride as our shared identity and toward a focus on self in an increasingly robust individualistic society.

Delbanco writes,

> Something died, or at least fell dormant, between the later 1960s, when the reform impulse subsided into solipsism, and the 1980s—two phases of our history that may seem far apart in political tone and personal style, but that finally cooperated in installing instant gratification as the hallmark of the good life, and in repudiating the interventions state as a source of hope. What was lost in the unholy alliance between an insouciant New Left and an insufferably smug New Right was any conception of a common destiny worth tears, sacrifice, and maybe even death.[13]

God and nation were both unifiers that existed outside the individual; as centers of gravity, they could hold people together as constellations. The third movement, individualism, is different. With individualism, the actual commitment is internal—self being the supreme value. This was reflected in language shifts from words such as *duty, service, sacrifice*, and *patriotism* to terms such as *self-realization, experience, commitment to happiness, personal growth*, and *self-expression*.

Delbanco tells us, "The history of hope I have tried to sketch . . . is one of diminution. At first, the self expanded toward—and was sometimes overwhelmed by—the vastness of God. From the early republic to the Great Society, it remained implicated in a national ideal lesser than God but larger and more enduring than any individual citizen. Today, hope has narrowed to the vanishing point of the self alone."[14]

The broad strokes Delbanco sketches are helpful. As is true with any characterization or generalization regarding groups or generations, nothing holds up as absolute or accurate across the board. However, these three historical mindsets do represent a large part of the changing experience and commitments of Americans through time.

They also represent three of the highest ideals we have as Americans: God, politics, self. These three ideas deeply form our very identity. In many ways they collectively make up our theology, or orthodoxy (right belief) and orthopraxy (right action). These three ideals are our American civil religion. This is why talking about religion or politics in just about any sector of US society is bound to elicit strong emotion, just as challenging an American's rights to privacy, autonomy, and freedom is bound to be met with a strong reaction.

These three categories provide an effective way of analyzing, critiquing, and framing a central truth in relation to race and privilege in America: racial equality and fairness is not just a good thing but an ideal that we must work toward if we are to fully realize Christian obedience, national justice, and individual flourishing.

The inequities in our system reflect problems with religious, political, and individual thinking over the centuries. Although not specifically in this order, I have sought in this book to address the categories of God, nation, and self in looking at privilege and responsibility. Exploring truth in each category can help us work toward a greater understanding, pursuit, and realization of equality.

In the past decade I have seen, in my own life and in the lives of those I have taught, how a deeper understanding of the gospel, racism in America, and our own formation leads to a reevaluation and reassessment of ideals, values, and theological convictions. Engaging more profoundly with the relational nature of the gospel, the systemic racism that has run in the veins of this country from its birth up to the present day, and the sociological underpinnings of our views of race and privilege can lead us into more authentic Christian love and spiritual witness.

May we gain the strength and sensitivity to have difficult conversations, even conversations about religion, politics, and cherished convictions, without pushing away from the dinner table.

CONCLUSION

> The task of prophetic ministry is to nurture, nourish, and evoke a
> consciousness and perception alternative to the consciousness
> and perception of the dominant culture around us.
>
> **WALTER BRUEGGEMANN,** *THE PROPHETIC IMAGINATION*

ON LOVING POLICE AND BELIEVING
BLACK LIVES MATTER

One of the greatest challenges I've faced the last few years has been
a commitment to continually bringing the tough conversation of race
and privilege before my church congregation.

It has meant throwing out sermons in order to address events dom-
inating the headlines and avoiding silence on issues the church needs
to think through and address.

One of the tension points in this conversation has been balancing
the emergence of the Black Lives Matter movement and the renewed
focus on police brutality with the presence and perspective of police
officers within our congregation.

Recently I sat down with a police officer who attends our church
to discuss his perspective on how Antioch handles the conversation.
It was a profitable and encouraging meeting for both of us. We were
able to agree on the deep complexity of America's racial injustices as
well as the dangers that can arise when we rush to judge others' actions.

Each of us heard the other say that both subjects matter: the value
of black and brown lives in America *and* the sacrifices made by police

officers and their families on behalf of the public good. If we talk only about one side, it can seem to imply that the other doesn't matter. The challenge is to make sure everyone is heard, understood, and valued.

My officer friend listened as I explained the challenge pastors face in trying to have difficult conversations when churches function more like social clubs than families. In families, we might disagree—even strongly—but we don't walk away from the dinner table. How do we talk about tough topics when people are trained not to converse but react?

I listened to his explanation of the challenges facing police officers in this highly politicized context, with increased disrespect for police while police lives are more at risk than any time he can remember. There are bad officers, just as in any profession—but the majority are good. They work hard, are asked to make incredibly difficult split-second decisions, and will still show up at our front door at two in the morning if our homes are threatened. While the majority of officers may be good, the system of policing is bigger than the individual, and the system may subvert even the best officer's intentions.

He simply wanted to know that I understood, and agreed with, the conviction that flipping from one extreme of dehumanization to another extreme—dehumanizing the police—doesn't lead us any closer to truth or realizing the love and equality God desires for us.

BECOMING JUST VERSUS DOING JUSTICE

My coffee meeting with this officer showed how easy and constructive difficult conversations can be if we commit to actually having them and hearing each other. It also reminded me just how difficult it is to pursue righteousness and justice. G. K. Chesterton once said, "There are an infinity of angles at which one falls, only one at which one stands."[1] Justice is a lot like that. It requires the effort of staying balanced in a world of tensions rather than swaying to one extreme or another.

And living with extremes and either-or categories often fits with a compartmentalized Christianity. We can become passionate about ending poverty in Malawi while ignoring poverty on Native American reservations.

Sex trafficking in Nepal can capture our hearts while we find no room in our hearts for the vulnerable girls or boys in our schools or in the foster care system.

The plight of refugees can grip us while we dismiss race issues as having to do more with politics than with justice.

If any part of justice matters then all of justice should matter. Being willing to open yourself up and engage in societal injustices is not easy, and it shouldn't be motivated primarily by guilt. Certainly, God's call is involved, and our capacity to hear it speaks to the magnitude of what we are or are not able to accomplish.

One of the major problems with the Pharisees in Jesus' day was not that there wasn't any good in them, but that they selectively chose to whom and not to whom or where and where not they would give of themselves.

We can become so cause driven that we subtly become like the Pharisees and hypocrites—dividing out who we love and who we are willing to sacrifice for and dismissing the rest. When we do, we lose balance and slide to the extremes.

And, as the writer of Ecclesiastes advised, "It is good to grasp the one and not let go of the other. Whoever fears God will avoid all extremes" (Ecclesiastes 7:18).

SLOWING DOWN

I'm an entrepreneur, and over the years I've started many projects and been involved with even more. It's taken a long time to realize, but I'm beginning to see that maybe I need to *do* less so I can *be* more.

Simply put, to live justly and righteously in all of life might require more of me than would be involved if I put on blinders and saw only one issue or one group of people.

Both ends and means matter. I need to pursue justice, but I also need to be just. I need to advocate for others, not forgetting the wounded on the road to Jericho because of my zeal for the engagement ahead—a neglect I've been guilty of at various times.

To be a good Samaritan is to have space for the wounded on the road to Jericho. To champion Jesus' form of integrated justice is not to save the world but to make space for the need of the other. Not only the predetermined need (what I would call a cause) but also the random, the overlooked, the nonsexy needs.

It took a long time on my justice journey for me to realize that the problem with justice is that I'm not very good at it. I'm good at tasks. I'm good at causes. I'm good at filling my schedule. But I'm not very good at justice.

To be good at justice—that is why I think I took on this book project.

To be good at justice means we often have to go slower rather than faster. The world is repaired more slowly than we expect, which means a whole lot of human suffering goes unresolved. There is so much to be lamented. Slower doesn't mean caring less; it means engaging more deeply. Slower doesn't mean things aren't urgent; it means they are too important to be glossed over or addressed with Band-Aids.

To be good at justice means we realize we are both a part of the solution and a part of the problem. Our actions complicate as well as fix the problems we see, which means a whole lot of the brokenness in this world results either from us or from systems we are complicit in or benefit from. There is much to be owned and repented of.

Justice isn't just about doing; it's about being. It isn't just about changing the world; it's also about changing ourselves.

And racism, possibly more than most, is a problem that sits in the messy middle. Not only is it hard to fix, but it requires a deep assessment and realigning of our own mental constructs, ways of viewing history, and notions of justice.

WHAT DIVIDES US?

I recently sat in Tel Aviv and listened to a discussion on peace and reconciliation by a Jewish woman and a Palestinian man. What made this talk different from other peacemaking conversations I had witnessed was that both had lost a child in the violence between Arabs and Jews.

The Jewish mother lost a son when a young Palestinian killed almost a dozen persons out of hatred and anger over the deaths of several of his uncles at the hands of Israelis.

The Palestinian father, in a gut-wrenching way, told how his ten-year-old daughter—walking with her sister in the schoolyard at 10 a.m., right after a math test—took a rubber bullet to the back of her head from an Israeli border patrol and died. (No doubt the patrol officer had his own story, his own fears, his own mistakes in a country where everyone bears personal pain and a complicated shared history.)

As the story unfolded, I wanted to leave the room. I had begun to cry and, as a father, couldn't take any more. I was in the chair directly next to the man, though, so I felt obligated to stay where I was. I'm glad I did, as the encounter of these two individuals turned out to be a life-changing moment for me.

This man, this woman, and hundreds of others have banded together into a "parents' circle." They have all chosen the path of peace rather than revenge. Each has determined to end the cycle of violence by forgiving, pitying, understanding, humanizing, and empathizing with the story of the other.

The Jewish mother said it well: "The beginning of the end of violence comes when we see the humanity in the other. The beginning of violence comes when we forget the humanity in the other."

Proximity comes from empathy, dignity, reconciliation, peace, and love.

Distance comes from objectification, labels, animosity, hatred, violence, and war.

Though they have suffered the direst loss, the parents in this Israeli-Palestinian parent circle live out love. They don't talk about peace, they make peace. They make peace with their choices. They make peace through their comfort and support of each other. They make peace every time they have to explain to family and community members why they are not seeking revenge. They make peace every time they choose to channel the pain not into destroying others but into creating beauty.

As the Palestianian father said in broken and heavily accented English, "I don't want to try revenge. Revenge doesn't work."

After a while, I began to think of my life against the backdrop of their story. I began to think about my family, my friends, and my community in relation to this story of reconciliation and redemption.

What divides us?

Gazing at the intense and sad eyes of this Palestinian father—a father who had to teach his thirteen-year-old son who wanted to be a warrior that he had not chosen peace out of weakness and that there is no shame in reconciliation—kept choking my lungs and constricting my throat with grief.

Against all this, what is it that divides us?

Oh Lord, forgive us for seeking comfort and prosperity rather than your kingdom.

Forgive us for killing your prophets.

Forgive us for defending the empire rather than railing against it with a prophetic voice.

Forgive us for centuries of cruelty, hardheartedness, and oppression.

Forgive us for ignoring your image.

Forgive us for prospering from the blood and tears of generations of your people.

SERVING BREAD

I opened this book with two quotes on one of the front leaves. The first, by President Calvin Coolidge, states, "To live under the American Constitution is the greatest political privilege that was ever accorded to the human race."

The second, popularly known as the Three-Fifths Clause, is taken from the US Constitution itself and highlights the position assigned

to Native Americans and enslaved persons, far below the white inhab-
itants of the colonies:

> Representatives and direct Taxes shall be apportioned among
> the several States which may be included within this Union,
> according to their respective Numbers, which shall be deter-
> mined by adding to the whole Number of free Persons, including
> those bound to Service for a Term of Years, and *excluding Indians*
> not taxed, *three fifths of all other Persons*. (United States Consti-
> tution, Article I, Section 2, Clause 3, emphasis added)

"All men are created equal." Those too are American words, but they
were written by aristocracy primarily for the privileged. We said them,
but we didn't believe them.

We are all created equal—no matter what race, color, or religion.

We now say these words, but do we believe them? And if we believe
them, is it only when it's comfortable or fits into categories of normalcy or standards we're accustomed to? Or do we believe them because people have dignity as beings made in the image of God, even
when our privilege feels threatened?

We have to challenge the impulse and aspiration toward aristocracy—
power and privilege permitting a life of leisure. We have to honor our
brothers and sisters and learn to make the common good part of our
aspirations. This goes against the grain of American individualism. It
cuts against our deep inclinations of self-realization and advancement.
Ultimately, it cuts against empire and the way we are shaped as consumers. The kingdom is a wholly different reality. None of us will get
it perfectly right, but we must be committed to that narrow road
where we are found in our love of enemy, love of neighbor, and life in
the communion of saints.

This isn't an easy vision. It is a prophetic vision that takes, as
Brueggemann wrote, a *prophetic imagination*. We should all have a
dream—not an American dream for our individual selves but a dream

for an America that reflects kingdom values and relationships as closely as possible.

No matter where you are—Oregon, Massachusetts, or Louisiana—what does it look like for you, your church, or your business to make space for the fullness of life in learning about, standing in solidarity with, and sacrificing for the other?

It's not how good or perfect you are at it—it's not a competition; it is how you are progressing or becoming. Are you, am I, willing to make sacrifices and elevate concern for the other?

Hospitality is defined as welcoming the other.

When we're in a posture of hospitality, we can't objectify those with whom we disagree. We can't throw stones while serving bread.

ACKNOWLEDGMENTS

I WANT TO THANK all those who have been gracious and patient with me as I have learned, and continue to learn, to walk toward justice.

Thank you to Leroy and Donna Barber for their encouragement, grace, and friendship.

Thank you also to Soong-Chan Rah, Lisa Sharon Harper, Troy Jackson, and Andy Smith for important phone calls and conversations about the framing of this project.

Thank you to my late friend Richard Twiss and to Mark Charles for helping me to better comprehend the Native American experience.

I would like to thank Rick Gerhardt, Ben Larson, and Mike Golafshar for their assistance in writing, specifically with chapters one, two, five, and six.

Emily Hill provided significant research on material throughout the book and especially helped with chapters four, eight, and nine. I would never have been able to complete this project without her support.

Adrianne Salmond contributed numerous edits and substantial help with citations, and Jarod Sickler provided research on the development of racism in philosophy.

Brian White, David Bailey, Mark Charles, Laura Wytsma, Linda VanVoorst, Paul Pastor, Roy Goble, and Jenny Yang all graciously provided helpful and insightful editorial reads.

Thank you also to the team at InterVarsity Press, and especially to Helen Lee and Al Hsu, for their commitment to bringing more books on race and privilege to Christian publishing.

APPENDIX

Recommended Reading

HERE I LIST BOOKS, historical and theological, Christian and non-Christian, recommended most often by leaders and experts in the area of race, diversity, and reconciliation. Use this list as a guide for you or your reading group to explore these topics further.

MOST HIGHLY RECOMMENDED BOOKS

Michelle Alexander, *The New Jim Crow: Mass Incarceration in the Age of Colorblindness*

Ta-Nehisi Coates, *Between the World and Me*

James H. Cone, *The Cross and the Lynching Tree*

Michael Emerson and Christian Smith, *Divided by Faith: Evangelical Religion and the Problem of Race in America*

Drew G. I. Hart, *Trouble I've Seen: Changing the Way the Church Views Racism*

Willie James Jennings, *The Christian Imagination: Theology and the Origins of Race*

Soong-Chan Rah, *The Next Evangelicalism: Freeing the Church from Western Cultural Captivity*

Bryan Stevenson, *Just Mercy: A Story of Justice and Redemption*

Beverly Tatum, *Why Are All the Black Kids Sitting Together in the Cafeteria?*

Howard Thurman, *Jesus and the Disinherited*

FURTHER RECOMMENDED READING

T. Carlos Anderson, *Just a Little Bit More: The Culture of Excess and the Fate of the Common Good*

Brian Bantum, *The Death of Race: Building a New Christianity in a Racial World*

Leroy Barber with Velma Maia Thomas, *Red, Brown, Yellow, Black, White— Who's More Precious in God's Sight? A Call for Diversity in Christian Missions and Ministry*

Dee Brown, *Bury My Heart at Wounded Knee: An Indian Story of the American West*

J. Cameron Carter, *Race: A Theological Account*

James H. Cone, *God of the Oppressed*

Mark DeYmaz, *Building a Healthy Multi-ethnic Church: Mandate, Commitments and Practices of a Diverse Congregation*

W. E. B. Du Bois, *The Souls of Black Folk*

Roxanne Dunbar-Ortiz, *An Indigenous Peoples' History of the United States*

Marian Wright Edelman, *The Sea Is So Wide and My Boat Is So Small: Charting a Course for the Next Generation*

Joe R. Feagin, *How Blacks Built America: Labor, Culture, Freedom, and Democracy*

Joe R. Feagin, *Racist America: Roots, Current Realities, and Future Reparations*

Joe R. Feagin, *The White Racial Frame: Centuries of Racial Framing and Counter-Framing*

Paulo Freire, *Pedagogy of the Oppressed*

Eduardo Galeano, *Open Veins of Latin America: Five Centuries of the Pillage of a Continent*

Gustavo Gutiérrez, *The Power of the Poor in History*

Lisa Sharon Harper, *The Very Good Gospel: How Everything Wrong Can Be Made Right*

Leslie J. Hoppe, *There Shall Be No Poor Among You: Poverty in the Bible*

Gish Jen, *Typical American* (fiction)

Emmanuel Katongole and Chris Rice, *Reconciling All Things: A Christian Vision for Justice, Peace and Healing*

Martin Luther King Jr., *Strength to Love*

Jonathan Kozol, *Savage Inequalities: Children in America's Schools*

Erika Lee, *The Making of Asian America*

Brenda Salter McNeil, *A Credible Witness: Reflections on Power, Evangelism, and Race*

Khalil Gibran Muhammad, *Condemnation of Blackness: Race, Crime, and the Making of Modern Urban America*

John Powell, *Racing to Justice: Transforming Our Conceptions of Self and Other to Build an Inclusive Society*

Daniel Rodriguez, *A Future for the Latino Church: Models for Multilingual, Multigenerational Hispanic Congregations*

Ron Takaki, *Strangers from a Different Shore: A History of Asian Americans*

Nikki Toyama-Szeto and Tracey Gee, eds., *More Than Serving Tea: Asian American Women on Expectations, Relationships, Leadership and Faith*

Richard Twiss, *Rescuing the Gospel from the Cowboys: A Native American Expression of the Jesus Way*

Chanequa Walker-Barnes, *Too Heavy a Yoke: Black Women and the Burden of Strength*

Jim Wallis, *America's Original Sin: Racism, White Privilege, and the Bridge to a New America*

Cornel West, *Race Matters*

Isabel Wilkerson, *The Warmth of Other Suns: The Epic Story of America's Great Migration*

Delores S. Williams, *Sisters in the Wilderness: The Challenge of Womanist God-Talk*

Tim Wise, *Under the Affluence: Shaming the Poor, Praising the Rich and Sacrificing the Future of America*

Tim Wise, *White like Me: Reflections on Race from a Privileged Son*

Frank Wu, *Yellow: Race in America Beyond Black and White*

Malcom X and Alex Haley, *The Autobiography of Malcolm X*

George Yancy, *Black Bodies, White Gazes: The Continuing Significance of Race*

Gene Luen Yang, *American Born Chinese* (graphic novel)

This list was compiled with recommendations from the following people: Samuel Adams, Vincent Bacote, Leroy Barber, Jonathan E. L. Brooks, Eugene Cho, Aaron Graham, Lisa Sharon Harper, Daniel Hill, Troy Jackson, Tyler Johnson, Helen Lee, Michael McBride, Alexia Salvatierra, Amy Williams, Jenny Yang.

NOTES

INTRODUCTION

[1]"U.S. Steps Closer to a Future Where Minorities Are the Majority," *Time*, June 24, 2015, http://time.com/3934092/us-population-diversity-census.

[2]Rahiel Tesfamariam, "My Experience of Racial Profiling at Chicago's Congress Plaza Hotel," *Urban Cusp*, June 8, 2015, www.urbancusp.com/2015/06/my-experience-of-racial-profiling-at-chicagos-congress-plaza-hotel/.

[3]Barna Group Research: Culture & Media, "Black Lives Matter and Racial Tension in America," May 5, 2016, https://barna.org/research/culture-media/research-release/black-lives-matter-and-racial-tension-in-america.

[4]This quote is attributed to Tim Wise, author of *White Like Me*, but it is uncertain whether this exact wording comes directly from him or is actually someone else's paraphrase of his perspectives. Cited in Sandhya Rani Jha, *Pre-Post-Racial America: Spiritual Stories from the Front Lines* (St. Louis, MO: Chalice, 2015), 109.

[5]Brooke Hempell, Barna Research Group: Culture & Media, "Black Lives Matter and Racial Tension in America." Respondents were asked if they agreed with the statement "Reverse racism, or prejudicial treatment of white people, is a problem in society today." Sixty-five percent agreed. Just over seven in ten white respondents afffirmed the statement, while black respondents feeling the same were fewer than half that number. Given that the Republican Party is 85 percent white, it really isn't a surprise that 77 percent of Republican respondents answered in the affirmative, while 53 percent of Democrats shared that opinion. (White people make up 54 percent of the Democratic Party's constituents.)

[6]Maya Angelou, *Letter to My Daughter* (New York: Random House, 2008), 65.

1 AMERICA'S WHITE STANDARD

[1]See U.S. Department of Justice, "Correctional Populations in the United States, 2014," December 2015, www.bjs.gov/content/pub/pdf/cpus14.pdf, and *Washington Post*, "Does the United States Really Have 5 Percent of the

World's Population and One Quarter of the World's Prisoners?," April 30, 2015, www.washingtonpost.com/news/fact-checker/wp/2015/04/30/does -the-united-states-really-have-five-percent-of-worlds-population-and -one-quarter-of-the-worlds-prisoners.

[2]An expression made more common after Jim Wallis's November 1987 *Sojourners* article "White Racism: America's Original Sin."

[3]Benjamin Franklin, "Observations Concerning the Increas of Mankind, Peopling of Countries, etc.," quoted in Roger Daniels, *Coming to America: A History of Immigration and Ethnicity in American Life*, 2nd ed. (New York: Harper Perennial, 2001), 110.

[4]Ibid.

[5]Ibid., 113.

[6]John Tehranian, "Performing Whiteness: Naturalization Litigation and the Construction of Racial Identity in America," *Yale Law Journal* 109 (2000): 819.

[7]Ibid., 819-20.

[8]Ibid., 820-21.

[9]Ibid., 819.

[10]Matthew Soerens and Jenny Hwang Yang, *Welcoming the Stranger: Justice, Compassion and Truth in the Immigration Debate* (Downers Grove, IL: Inter-Varsity Press, 2009), 52.

[11]Daniels, *Coming to America*, 245.

[12]Soerens and Yang, *Welcoming the Stranger*, 53.

[13]Ibid., 54.

[14]Ibid.

[15]Ibid.

[16]Daniels, *Coming to America*, 329.

[17]In this discussion, I have referred to America as a melting pot, as it has been for many years. In fact, the idea of a melting pot has now become the idea of a salad bowl in which, instead of melting together and co-alescing, various races are sticking to their cultures but are still able to live together harmoniously.

[18]Soerens and Yang, *Welcoming the Stranger*, 57-58.

[19]Soong-Chan Rah, interview by the author, April 29, 2016.

[20]Richard Rohr, "Richard Rohr on White Privilege," interview by Romal Tune, *Huffington Post*, January 15, 2016, www.huffingtonpost.com/romal-tune /richard-rohr-on-white-pri_b_8985742.html.

2 WHEN THE WORLD BECAME RACIST

[1]Winfried Corduan, *In the Beginning God: A Fresh Look at the Case for Original Monotheism* (Nashville: B&H Publishing, 2013), 52.

[2]Pascal Gagneux et al., "Mitochondrial Sequences Show Diverse Evolutionary Histories of African Hominoids," *Proceedings of the National Academy of Sciences, USA* 96 (1999): 5077-82; Bruce Bower, "Chimps Outdo People in Genetic Diversity," *Science News* 156 (1999): 295.

[3]Mary-Claire King and Arno G. Motulsky, "Mapping Human History," *Science* 298 (2002): 2342-43; Noah A. Rosenberg et al., "Genetic Structure of Human Populations," *Science* 298 (2002): 2381-85.

[4]Sandra Beleza et al., "The Timing of Pigmentation Lightening in Europeans," *Molecular Biology and Evolution* 30 (2013): 24-35.

[5]See, e.g., Catherine M. S. Alexander and Stanley King, *Shakespeare and Race* (Cambridge: Cambridge University Press, 2000).

[6]George Kirkpatrick Hunter, "Elizabethans and Foreigners," *Shakespeare Survey* 17 (1964): 37-52.

[7]Andrew Valls, introduction to *Race and Racism in Modern Philosophy*, ed. Andrew Valls (Ithaca, NY: Cornell University Press, 2005), 5.

[8]David Hume, "Essay XXI: Of National Characters," in *Essays, Moral, Political, and Literary* (1777), 207n, available at http://oll.libertyfund.org/titles/hume -essays-moral-political-literary-lf-ed.

[9]Quoted in Emmanuel Eze, "The Color of Reason: The Idea of 'Race' in Kant's Anthropology," in *Postcolonial African Philosophy: A Critical Reader*, ed. Emmanuel Eze (Oxford: Blackwell, 1997), 103-40.

[10]Ibid., 122.

[11]Robert Bernasconi, "Kant as an Unfamiliar Source of Racism," in *Philosophers on Race: Critical Essays*, ed. Julie K. Ward and Tommy L. Lott (Oxford: Blackwell, 2002), 159.

[12]Philip T. Hoffman, *Why Did Europe Conquer the World?* (Princeton, NJ: Princeton University Press, 2015), 2.

[13]Thomas Cahill, *Heretics and Heroes: How Renaissance Artists and Reformation Priests Created Our World* (New York: Anchor Books, 2014), 64-65.

[14]"Race," in *Online Etymology Dictionary*, www.etymonline.com/index.php?term =race&allowed_in_frame=0, accessed May 21, 2016.

[15]Pope Alexander VI, *Inter Caetera*, May 4, 1493. An English translation can be accessed at www.let.rug.nl/usa/documents/before-1600/the-papal-bull-inter -caetera-alexander-vi-may-4-1493.php.

[16]Cahill, *Heretics and Heroes*, 56-57.

[17]Ibid., 58-59.

[18]Suggested reading: David Stannard, *American Holocaust*; Dee Brown and Hampton Sides, *Bury My Heart at Wounded Knee*; James Wilson, *The Earth Shall Weep*; Peter Nabikov and Vine Deloria, *Native American Testimony*.

[19]See Mark Charles and Soong-Chan Rah's forthcoming book on the doctrine of discovery.

[20]*Johnson v. McIntosh*, 21 U.S. 543. Case brief can be accessed at www.casebriefs .com/blog/law/property/property-law-keyed-to-cribbet/role-of-property-in -society/johnson-v-mcintosh.

[21]Richard Twiss, *One Church, Many Tribes* (Ventura, CA: Regal Books, 2000), 47-48.

[22]R. Pierce Beaver, *The Native American Christian Community: A Directory of Indian, Aleut, and Eskimo Churches* (Monrovia, CA: MARC, 1979), 31, 46. Quoted in Twiss, *One Church, Many Tribes*, 26.

3 STOLEN LABOR

[1]W. E. B. Du Bois, *Black Reconstruction in America 1860-1880* (New York: Simon and Schuster, 1935), 30.

[2]C. Vann Woodward, *The Strange Career of Jim Crow*, commemorative ed. (Oxford: Oxford University Press, 2001), 7.

[3]Jerrold M. Packard, *American Nightmare* (New York: St. Martin's, 2002), 65.

[4]Woodward, *Strange Career of Jim Crow*, 7.

[5]Packard, *American Nightmare*, 76.

[6]Ibid., 79.

[7]David M. Oshinsky, *Worse Than Slavery: Parchman Farm and the Ordeal of Jim Crow Justice* (New York: Simon and Schuster, 1996), 20.

[8]Michelle Alexander, *The New Jim Crow: Mass Incarceration in the Age of Colorblindness* (New York: New Press, 2010), 28.

[9]W. E. B. Du Bois, "Reconstruction and Its Benefits," *American Historical Review* 15, no. 4 (1910): 784.

[10]Oshinsky, *Worse Than Slavery*, 41.

[11]Ibid., 44.

[12]Douglas A. Blackmon, "From Alabama's Past, Capitalism Teamed with Racism to Create Cruel Partnership," *Wall Street Journal*, July 26, 2001, www .wsj.com/articles/SB995228253461746936.

[13]Ibid.

[14]Oshinsky, *Worse Than Slavery*, 47.

[15]Blackmon, "From Alabama's Past, Capitalism Teamed with Racism."

[16]Oshinsky, *Worse Than Slavery*, 67.

[17]Blackmon, "From Alabama's Past, Capitalism Teamed with Racism."

[18]Oshinsky, *Worse Than Slavery*, 47.

[19]Ibid.

[20]Ibid., 58.

[21]Blackmon, "From Alabama's Past, Capitalism Teamed with Racism."

[22]Oshinsky, *Worse Than Slavery*, 60.

[23]See the epilogue in Douglas A. Blackmon's *Slavery by Another Name* (New York: Anchor Books, 2008).

[24]Ibid., 396.

[25]Ibid., 4-5.

[26]Ibid., 402.

[27]Ibid.

[28]Richard H. Pildes, "Democracy, Anti-Democracy, and the Canon," *Constitutional Commentary* 17, no. 295 (2000): 299-301.

[29]Ibid., 303-4.

[30]Mary Ann Glendon, *A World Made New: Eleanor Roosevelt and the Universal Declaration of Human Rights* (New York: Random House Trade Paperbacks, 2001), 36.

[31]Tom LoBianco, "Report: Aide Says Nixon's War on Drugs Targeted Blacks, Hippies," CNN, March 24, 2016, www.cnn.com/2016/03/23/politics/john-ehrlichman-richard-nixon-drug-war-blacks-hippie/index.html.

[32]James Boyd, "Nixon's Southern Strategy: 'It's All in the Charts,'" *New York Times*, May 17, 1970, www.nytimes.com/packages/html/books/phillips-southern .pdf, accessed July 25, 2012.

[33]Ibid.

[34]Nicolas Lemann, *The Promised Land: The Great Black Migration and How It Changed America* (New York: Vintage Books, 1991), 203-4.

[35]See Rick Perlstein, "Exclusive: Lee Atwater's Infamous 1981 Interview on the Southern Strategy," *Nation*, November 13, 2012, www.thenation.com /article/exclusive-lee-atwaters-infamous-1981-interview-southern-strategy/, accessed April 12, 2016.

[36]Alexander, *New Jim Crow*, 12.

[37]Richard Nixon, press conference, June 18, 1971, the day after he presented a document to Congress called "Drug Abuse and Control."

[38]Alexander, *New Jim Crow*, 50.

[39]Ibid., 49.

[40]Ibid., 51.

[41]Ibid., 52.

[42]Ibid., 55.

[43]Ibid., 53.

[44]Ibid., 58.

[45]Christopher Ingraham, "White People Are More Likely to Deal Drugs, but Black People Are More Likely to Get Arrested for It," *Washington Post*, September 30, 2014, www.washingtonpost.com/news/wonk/wp/2014/09/30 /white-people-are-more-likely-to-deal-drugs-but-black-people-are-more -likely-to-get-arrested-for-it.

[46]Ibid.

[47]Alexander, *New Jim Crow*, 78.

[48]Ibid., 89.

[49]Ibid., 85.

[50]Ibid., 86.

[51]Ibid., 141-77.

[52]Ibid., 184.

[53]Ibid., 180.

[54]Jeff Guo, "America Has Locked Up So Many Black People It Has Warped Our Sense of Reality," *Washington Post*, February 26, 2016, www.washingtonpost .com/news/wonk/wp/2016/02/26/america-has-locked-up-so-many-black -people-it-has-warped-our-sense-of-reality/.

[55]Sentencing Project, "US Prison Population Trends 1999-2014: Broad Variations in States in Recent Years," February 2016, http://sentencingproject .org/doc/publications/inc_US_Prison_Population_Trends_1999-2014.pdf.

4 HOW OUR CITIES GOT THEIR SHAPE

[1]Ira Berlin, *The Making of African America: The Four Great Migrations* (New York: Penguin Books, 2010), 9.

[2]Isabel Wilkerson, *The Warmth of Other Suns: The Epic Story of America's Great Migration* (New York: Random House, 2010), 10.

[3]Berlin, *Making of African America*, 152-53.

[4]Nicholas Lemann, *The Promised Land: The Great Black Migration and How It Changed America* (New York: Random House, 1991), 16.

[5]Ibid.

[6]Wilkerson, *Warmth of Other Suns*, 39.

[7]Ibid., 217.

[8]Berlin, *Making of African America*, 161-62.

[9]Lemann, *Promised Land*, 49.

[10]Berlin, *Making of African America*, 156.

[11]Wilkerson, *Warmth of Other Suns*, 178.

[12]Berlin, *Making of African America*, 191.

[13]Ibid., 183.

[14]Ibid., 197.

[15]Ibid., 198-99.

[16]Wilkerson, *Warmth of Other Suns*, 529.

[17]Berlin, *Making of African America*, 200.

[18]Lemann, *Promised Land*, 91.

[19]Frank Capra, dir., *It's a Wonderful Life*, DVD (orig. 1946; Los Angeles: Republic Pictures, 2001).

[20]"Homestead Act—Homestead National Monument of America" (U.S. National Park Service), www.nps.gov/home/learn/historyculture/abouthomesteadactlaw.htm, accessed May 24, 2016.

[21]Christine Herbes-Sommers, Tracy Heather Straing, and Llewellyn M. Smith, "The House We Live In," episode 3 of the documentary *Race: The Power of Illusion*, PBS, 2003.

[22]"Time to Bring Back the Home Owners Loan Corporation?," Roosevelt Institute, August 31, 2010, http://rooseveltinstitute.org/time-bring-back-home-owners-loan-corporation/.

[23]Herbes-Sommers, Straing, and Smith, "House We Live In."

[24]Ta-Nehisi Coates, "The Case for Reparations," *Atlantic*, June 2014, www.theatlantic.com/magazine/archive/2014/06/the-case-for-reparations/361631/, accessed December 12, 2014.

[25]"FHA Underwriting Manual, Rev. Apr. 1, 1936," Urbanoasis.org, http://urbanoasis.org/projects/fha/FHAUnderwritingManualPtl.html, accessed May 25, 2016.

[26]Frederik Heller, "The Code Hits 100," *Realtor Magazine* (National Association for Realtors), November 2012, http://realtormag.realtor.org/law-and-ethics/ethics/article/2012/11/code-hits-100, accessed December 13, 2014.

[27]Coates, "Case for Reparations."

[28]Ibid.

[29]Ibid.

[30]Mike Golafshar, personal communication.

[31]Coates, "Case for Reparations."

[32]United States Commission on Civil Rights, "Hearing Held in St. Louis, Missouri, Jan. 14-17, 1970."

[33]The Urban Institute, "Nine Charts About Wealth Inequality in America," February 2015, http://apps.urban.org/features/wealth-inequality-charts.

[34]Ibid.

[35]Although such laws were not unique to Oregon, this brief list of Oregon laws exemplifies the challenges Native Americans faced and migrants and immigrants had to navigate in relocating to the Northwest during its formative years:

The 1844 Organic Act made it illegal for African Americans or mulattos to come to Oregon; the penalty for doing so was being sold at auction to the lowest bidder.

The 1850 Federal Oregon Donation Land Act let (white) non-Indians stake a claim on land whether or not Indians lived on it. It barred African Americans from staking any claims and voided previous acts protecting Indians and their land titles.

1853–1855: All land titles in the Willamette Valley were codified, and Indian tribes were moved to two reservations.

1855: Law passed prevented mixed-race males from becoming citizens.

1857: Bill passed assessing a mining tax on Chinese.

1860: Bill passed assessing tax for Chinese to engage in business.

1862: Bill passed assessing poll tax on African Americans, Asians, and Pacific Islanders.

1863: African Americans were excluded from jury duty.

1864: It became illegal to entice an Indian to leave the reservation.

1923: Alien Land Law prevented first-generation Japanese from owning or leasing land; business licenses were also refused to first-generation Japanese.

For more information, see www.oregonencyclopedia.org/articles/exclusion _laws/#.V04H5Id9jaM and www.ode.state.or.us/opportunities/grants/saelp /orraciallaws.pdf.

5 THE ARISTOCRATIC ITCH

[1]James Egner, "A Bit of Britain Where the Sun Still Never Sets: 'Downton Abbey' Reaches Around the World," *New York Times,* January 3, 2013, www .nytimes.com/2013/01/06/arts/television/downton-abbey-reaches-around -the-world.html, accessed September 12, 2016.

[2]Viviane Rutabingwa and James Kasaga Arinaitwe, "Taylor Swift Is Dreaming of a Very White Africa," *Goats and Soda: Stories of Life in a Changing World*, NPR, September 1, 2015, www.npr.org/sections/goatsandsoda/2015/09/01/436653602/taylor-swift-is-dreaming-of-a-very-white-africa.

[3]J. T. Adams, *The Epic of America* (Garden City, NY: Blue Ribbon Books, 1941), 404.

[4]dennisw, Free Republic, July 7, 2015, www.freerepublic.com/focus/news/3308621/posts, accessed August 20, 2016.

[5]Anthony B. Bradley, "The Kingdom Today," in *The Kingdom of God*, ed. Christopher W. Morgan and Robert A. Peterson, Theology in Community (Wheaton, IL: Crossway, 2012), Kindle ed., chap. 9.

[6]Walter Brueggemann, "Discussion of the Prophetic Imagination," lecture, Kilns College, Bend, OR, September 28, 2015.

[7]Ibid.

[8]Brueggemann lays out his definition and discussion of the royal consciousness in chapter 2 of *The Prophetic Imagination*, 2nd ed. (Minneapolis: Fortress, 2001), 21.

[9]Brueggemann, "Discussion of the Prophetic Imagination."

[10]Timothy Keller, *Generous Justice: How God's Grace Makes Us Just* (New York: Dutton, 2010), 5.

[11]N. T. Wright, *Surprised by Hope: Rethinking Heaven, the Resurrection, and the Mission of the Church* (San Francisco: HarperOne, 2008), 264.

6 DOES JUSTICE BELONG IN OUR GOSPEL CONVERSATION?

[1]Nicholas Wolterstorff, *Justice: Rights and Wrongs* (Princeton, NJ: Princeton University Press, 2008), viii-ix.

[2]Gustavo Gutiérrez, *A Theology of Liberation: History, Politics and Salvation* (Maryknoll, NY: Orbis Books, 1973), 232.

[3]Ignacio Ellacuría, *Essays on History, Liberation, and Salvation* (Maryknoll, NY: Orbis Books, 2013).

7 THE SALVATION INDUSTRIAL COMPLEX

[1]Examples of such language: Romans 8:1; 2 Corinthians 5:19; Ephesians 1:1, 20; Philippians 1:1; Colossians 1:2; 1 Thessalonians 4:16.

[2]G. K. Chesterton, *What I Saw in America* (New York: Dodd and Mead and Company, 1923; London: Catholic Way Publishing, 2013), 269, emphasis added.

[3]Lisa Sharon Harper, *The Very Good Gospel: How Everything Wrong Can Be Made Right* (Colorado Springs: WaterBrook, 2016), 7.

[4]W. J. de Kock, *Out of My Mind: Following the Trajectory of God's Regeneration Story* (Eugene, OR: Wipf and Stock, 2014), 4.

[5]Reggie Williams, *Bonhoeffer's Black Jesus: Harlem Renaissance Theology and an Ethic of Resistance* (Waco, TX: Baylor University Press, 2014), 139.

[6]Ibid.

[7]Dietrich Bonhoeffer, *Dietrich Bonhoeffer Works*, vol. 4, *Discipleship* (Minneapolis: Augsburg Fortress, 2001), 78-79.

[8]Ibid., 79.

[9]Ibid.

8 A SHORT LOOK AT AMERICAN INDIVIDUALISM

[1]Alexis de Tocqueville, *Democracy in America*, ed. J. P. Mayer, trans. George Lawrence (New York: Anchor, 1969), 692.

[2]Gary Deddo, "Persons in Racial Reconciliation: The Contributions of a Trinitarian Theological Anthropology," in *The Gospel in Black and White*, ed. Dennis L. Okholm (Downers Grove, IL: InterVarsity Press, 1997), 65.

[3]Martin Luther King Jr., Clayborne Carson, and Peter Holloran, *A Knock at Midnight: Inspiration from the Great Sermons of Reverend Martin Luther King, Jr.* (New York: Intellectual Properties Management and Warner Books, 1998), 85.

[4]Soong-Chan Rah, "The Sin of Racism: Racialization of the Image of God," in *The Image of God in an Image Driven Age: Explorations in Theological Anthropology*, ed. Beth Felker Jones and Jeffrey W. Barbeau (Downers Grove, IL: InterVarsity Press, 2016), 206-7.

9 WHEN RACISM WENT UNDERGROUND

[1]Barna Group, "Black Lives Matter and Racial Tension in America," May 5, 2016, www.barna.com/research/black-lives-matter-and-racial-tension-in-america/.

[2]Bryon Rossi, email message to author, April 21, 2016. You can find the searchable database at http://photogrammar.yale.edu.

[3]Cheryl Staats, Kelly Capatasto, Robin A. Wright, and Danya Contractor, "State of the Science: Implicit Bias Review 2015," Kirwan Institute for Race and Ethnicity, http://kirwaninstitute.osu.edu/wp-content/uploads/2015/05/2015-kirwan-implicit-bias.pdf, 62, accessed May 16, 2016.

⁴Ibid.

⁵Kirwan Institute at Ohio State University has been publishing an annual review of research on implicit bias since 2013. For the detailed 2015 review, see http://kirwaninstitute.osu.edu/wp-content/uploads/2015/05/2015-kirwan -implicit-bias.pdf.

⁶Staats et al., "State of the Science," 63.

⁷Nicholas Kristof, "When Whites Just Don't Get It, Part 6," *New York Times*, April 2, 2016, www.nytimes.com/2016/04/03/opinion/sunday/when-whites -just-dont-get-it-part-6.html, accessed May 11, 2016.

⁸Claude M. Steele, *Whistling Vivaldi: How Stereotypes Affect Us and What We Can Do* (New York: W. W. Norton, 2010), 6-7.

⁹Hazel Trice Edney, "New 'Doll Test' Produces Ugly Results," *Saint Louis American*, August 24, 2006, www.stlamerican.com/entertainment/living_it /article_3e9a2dfd-816b-560b-bdb6-a2a58aeda848.html.

¹⁰"Hear the 911 Call About Tamir Rice: Gun Is 'Probably Fake,' Caller Says," *Los Angeles Times*, November 26, 2014, www.latimes.com/nation/nationnow /la-na-nn-tamir-rice-911-call-20141126-htmlstory.html.

¹¹Jeah Lee, "How Cleveland Police May Have Botched a 911 Call Before Killing Tamir Rice," *Mother Jones*, June 25, 2015, www.motherjones.com /politics/2015/06/tamir-rice-police-killing-911-call-investigation.

¹²"Whites More Likely to Misidentify Tools as Guns When Linked to Black Faces," *Ohio State University Research News*, https://researchnews.osu.edu /archive/gunbias.htm, accessed May 10, 2016.

¹³Willie James Jennings, *The Christian Imagination: Theology and the Origins of Race* (New Haven, CT: Yale University Press, 2010), 35.

¹⁴Kristof, "When Whites Just Don't Get It, Part 6."

¹⁵Staats et al., "State of the Science," 65-66.

¹⁶Christena Cleveland, *Disunity in Christ: Uncovering the Hidden Forces That Keep Us Apart* (Downers Grove, IL: InterVarsity Press, 2013), 63.

10 THE VOICE OF JUSTICE

¹Much of the following is borrowed from an article I wrote for the *Huffington Post*. Ken Wytsma, "Richard Twiss, Speaking Plain Truth and Promoting Diversity at Christian Conferences," *Huffington Post*, April 3, 2013, www .huffingtonpost.com/ken-wytsma/richard-twiss-speaking-plain-truth-and -promoting-diversity-at-christian-conferences_b_2903128.html.

²James H. Cone, *The Cross and the Lynching Tree* (Marynoll, NY: Orbis Books, 2011), 62.

[3]"Nonprofit Funding Bias and Diversity in Foundations," UrbanMinistry .org, www.urbanministry.org/foundationdiversity, accessed May 17, 2016.

[4]Christena Cleveland, *Disunity in Christ: Uncovering the Hidden Forces That Keep Us Apart* (Downers Grove, IL: InterVarsity Press, 2013), 41.

[5]"Nonprofit Funding Bias and Diversity in Foundations," UrbanMinistry .org, accessed May 10, 2016.

[6]Leroy Barber with Velma Maia Thomas, *Red, Brown, Yellow, Black, White— Who's More Precious in God's Sight? A Call for Diversity in Christian Missions and Ministry* (New York: Jericho Books, 2014), 44.

[7]Ibid., 50.

[8]W. J. de Kock, *Out of My Mind: Following the Trajectory of God's Regeneration Story* (Eugene, OR: Wipf and Stock, 2014), 82.

[9]Miroslav Volf, *Exclusion and Embrace: A Theological Exploration of Identity, Otherness, and Reconciliation* (Nashville: Abingdon, 1996), 129.

[10]Cleveland, *Disunity in Christ*, 170.

[11]Barber, *Red, Brown, Yellow, Black, White*, 57-58.

11 FINDING OURSELVES IN THE OTHER

[1]Joseph Stiglitz, *The Great Divide: Unequal Societies and What We Can Do About Them* (New York: W. W. Norton, 2015), 160.

[2]Stanley Hauerwas, *In Good Company: The Church as Polis* (Notre Dame, IN: University of Notre Dame Press, 1995), 157.

[3]Walter Brueggemann, *Journey to the Common Good* (Louisville, KY: Westminster John Knox, 2010), 26.

[4]Soong-Chan Rah, in Mary Elise Cannon, Lisa Sharon Harper, Troy Jackson, and Soong-Chan Rah, *Forgive Us: Confessions of a Compromised Faith* (Grand Rapids: Zondervan, 2014), 27.

[5]John Dawson, *Healing America's Wounds* (Ventura, CA: Regal Books, 1996), 30.

[6]Conversation with Soong-Chan Rah, April 29, 2016.

[7]Interestingly enough, I learned some hard lessons even in this experience. While my heart was in the right place, by bringing Alexia into my slot I was still demonstrating a power differential. Alexia is a recognized leader in the field; I should have used my power in the behind-the-scenes planning and strategizing to give Alexia her own slot to speak—not as a voice occupying my time and at the end of my invitation.

[8]Adam Hochschild, *King Leopold's Ghost: A Story of Greed, Terror, and Heroism in Colonial Africa* (New York: Mariner Books / Houghton Mifflin, 1999), 233.

[9]Ibid., 277.

[10]Ibid.

[11]Delbanco cites this in reference to the transition from religion to nation. Walt Whitman, preface to *Leaves of Grass*, in *Whitman: Complete Poetry and Collected Prose*, ed. Justin Kaplan (New York: Literary Classics of the United States, 1982), 5.

[12]For others, such as Japanese Americans confined to internment camps, World War II was a painful experience of American nationalism.

[13]Andrew Delbanco, *The Real American Dream: A Meditation on Hope* (Cambridge, MA: Harvard University Press, 1999), 97.

[14]Ibid., 103.

CONCLUSION

[1]G. K. Chesterton, *Orthodoxy*, in *The Collected Works of G. K. Chesterton* (San Francisco: Ignatius Press, 1986), 1:306.

INDEX

abolition movement, 123
African Americans, 16, 24,
    58-59
    barred access to
        programs, 74
    black codes, 51
    blackness redefined, 68
    cycles of defeat, 54
    experience of, 67-68
    incarceration rates, 64
    living in cities, 70
    lynching, 69
    migration, 56
    mortality rates, 36,
        52-53
    oppression of, 56-57, 60
    president, 21
    voting rights, 48, 55-56
age of discovery, 39
age of exploration, 24, 32,
    36
Alexander, Michelle, 61-62
America's original sin, 12
American dream, 73, 86, 88,
    169-70, 181
American ethics, 125
aristocracy, 85, 90, 93
    British ranks, 87
    nobility, 86
    peerage, 86
Asian Americans, 17-18,
    21-22
Atwater, Lee, 59
Barber, Leroy, 159, 165-66
Barna Group, 5
Belgian Congo, 178
Berlin, Ira, 67, 71
bias, 80
    implicit, 140-45
    subconscious, 133, 139,
        150-51

Black Lives Matter
    movement, 168-69, 185
Blackmon, Douglas, 54-55
Bonhoeffer, Dietrich,
    124-26
Booth, John Wilkes, 47
Bright, Bill, 117
*Brown v. Board of
    Education of Topeka,*
    49-50, 144
Brueggemann, Walter,
    90-91, 94, 173, 185
Cahill, Thomas, 36, 40-41
California, 15-17
    Alien Land Law (1920),
        14
Calvinism, 123
Catholic Church, 39,
    148-49, 153
census, 15, 18
Charleston church
    shooting, 98
Chicago, 3, 68-70, 75-77
    Bronzeville, 71
    Commission on Race
        Relations, 69
    south side, 72
Chief Joseph Brant, 43
Chinese, 15, 206
    Exclusion Act, 16
Christian conferences,
    154-57
civil rights, 18, 50, 54, 56
Civil Rights Act of 1964,
    56
Civil War, 13, 47, 50, 54, 73,
    137-38, 179
Clark, Ken and Mamie, 50
class distinction, 157
class mobility, 36

Cleveland, Christena, 158,
    166
cocaine. *See* war on drugs
Code of Ethics (1924), 75
Cold War, 56-57
colonialism
    act of establishing
        colonies, 36, 38, 44,
        85, 178
    Belgian, 178
    exploitation in, 32
    justification of, 39
colorblindness, 23, 63-64
Columbus, Christopher,
    39-40
Communion, 164-65
compassion ministries, 162
Cone, James, 67, 157-58
Confederate states, 55
confession, 176
conversion. *See* salvation
convict leasing, 50-53,
    54-55, 63
creation story, 168, 176
creativity
    and imagination, 91-92
    and justice, 105, 163
Daley, Richard J., 72
de Kock, Wynand, 163-64
Declaration of
    Independence, 39
Delbanco, Andrew, 181-82
Democratic Party, 47, 58
demonization, 18
desegregation in schools,
    70
discrimination, 55
disenfranchisement, 48, 55
dispensational theology,
    103-5
diversity, 31

doctrines of discovery, 39-40, 42
doll test, 50, 144
drug use rates, 62
D'Souza, Dinesh, 12, 26
Elizabethan England, 32-33
emancipation, 45
empire, 36, 90
Enforcement Acts, 48
equality, 45, 131, 191
Erlichman, John, 57-58
ethnic diversity, 157
Eucharist. *See* Communion
exclusionary laws, 79
exploitation, 75-76
Fair Employment Practices Commission, 70
Fair Housing Act (1968), 78
Fair Sentencing Act (2010), 61
faith, 171
Federal Housing Authority (FHA), 73
Fifteenth Amendment, 48, 55
Finney, Charles, 118, 123
First Great Awakening, 121
forty acres and a mule, 179
foundations boards, make up of, 158-59
Fourteenth Amendment, 49
Franklin, Benjamin, 13
freedom of speech, 23
Freedom Ride of 1961, 57
genetics, 31-32
genocide, 38
Germany, 36
ghetto, 75
God, 164-65
    color of, 148
    communal image of, 130
    image of, 19, 35, 79, 131, 148

gold rush, 15, 68
golden rule, 124-25
gospel, 110-12
grace, 124
Great Depression, 73-74
Great Migration. *See* migration
Great Reversal, 103-4
Greatest Generation, 181
group righteousness, 96-97
groupthink, 158
guilt, 162
Harlem, 71, 125
Hauerwas, Stanley, 170-71
hierarchy, 80-81
historical sin, 23
Historically Black Colleges and Universities (HBCUs), 23-24, 167-68
Hollywood, 57
Holocaust, 149
Holy Spirit, 164-65, 180
Home Owner's Loan Corp (HOLC), 73-74
homeownership, 72-74, 78
Homestead Act (1862), 73
identity, 167-68, 170
    cultural, 176
    individual, 182
    under God, 182
imago Dei. See God: image of
immigration, 13-18
implicit bias, 146-47
Indians. *See* Native Americans
indigenous people, 155
individualism, 129-30, 182
industrial centers, 70
industrialization, 69
inequality, 61-62, 86
injustice, 56
inner cities, 60
International African Association, 178
Jennings, Willie James, 85, 150

Jesus, 164-65
    asking into heart, 118-21 (*see also* salvation)
    cross as a bridge, 117
Jews, 149
Jim Crow, 24, 49-51, 55-57, 61, 63, 69, 80, 144, 169
Johnson, Lyndon B., 18, 59
Johnson v. McIntosh, 42
justice, 4, 101-3, 107, 147
    as a cause, 162
    equitable, 64
    holistic, 161
    primary, 108
    pursuit of, 185-87
    restorative, 109
    social, 153
Justice Conference, The, 19, 102, 161, 177
King, Martin Luther, Jr., 131, 142
Ku Klux Klan, 19
lament, 41
liberation theology, 153-54
liberty, 56
Lincoln, Abraham, 47-48, 73
Luther, Martin, 110
lynching, 69
making space, 163-64
mandatory sentencing, 61
Manifest Destiny, 45
marijuana, 60, 64
    See also war on drugs
Marshall, Thurgood, 42, 49, 144
Martin, Trayvon, 146-47
McCarran-Walter Act (1952), 16, 18
melting pot, 17-18
Mexican-American War, 15
Michelangelo, 148-49
Middle Ages, 37-38
migration
    Great Migration, 68-72, 78, 141

Great Northern Drive, 68-69
minorities, 22
Mother's Day bus bombing, 57
NAACP, 56
National Association of Real Estate Board, 75
Native Americans, 42-44, 154, 156, 180
naturalization, 13-15
New Deal, 73
new world, 39-40, 42
Nixon, Richard, 57-59
nonprofit funding, 158-59
North, 49, 68
Pacific Northwest, 78-79
Palestine, 149
paternalism, 158
peerage. *See* aristocracy
penitentiary, 51
Philips, Kevin, 58-59
philosophers, 34, 149
plea bargains, 63
Plessy v. Ferguson, 49
police brutality, 3-4, 185
political agenda, 5
poverty, 141
preferential treatment, 2-3, 20
prejudice, 37, 44
premillennialism, 104
primates, 31
prisoners, 51
privilege, 3, 6, 22, 24-26, 90-91, 139, 162-63
    dismantling of, 180
property contract, 75-76
property ownership, 14
prophetic word, 94-95
Protestants, 21
public defender, availability of, 63
race, 32, 37-38, 80
    bias regarding, 4-5
    disparities between, 54

as seen in early cultures, 37
    grouping by, 14
    human, 45
    profiling of, 3, 62
    relations, 171
    and skin color, 45
    theology of, 22
racism, 6, 21-23, 26-27, 29-30, 34, 38, 72, 138
    reverse, 2
Rah, Soong-Chan, 47, 65, 131, 173, 175
railroads
    building, 51
    Central Pacific Railroad, 15
    Illinois Central Railroad, 69
reparations, 179-80
Rasmus, Rudy, 168-69
Reconstruction, 48-49, 51
Reconstruction Acts of 1867, 55
RED movement, 161
redlining, 74, 78
Relocation Act, 42
Republican Party, 58
restoration, 176
Rice, Tamir, 145
righteousness, 106-8, 110-11
Rooney Rule, 166
salvation, 118-23
    alter call, 118
    Sinner's Prayer, 118, 123, 127
    transactional versus relational, 126
segregation, 13, 49, 50, 56, 72, 75, 80, 165
separate but equal, 49
sex trafficking, 161
Shakespeare, William, 32-33
sharecropper system, 69
Sherman, William T., 179

silver rule, 124-25
sin nature, 45
slave trade, 13, 38
slavery, 14, 32, 44, 63, 80, 138, 161
    belief system, 48
    end of, 54
    state-sponsored, 56
South (US), 47, 68-69, 86, 179
South Africa, 179
Soviet Union, 57
Stanley, Henry Morton, 178
states' rights, 59, 137-38
stereotypes, 34
systems of oppression, 48
Tocqueville, Alexis de, 129-30
Twiss, Richard, 42-44, 154-56
Union, 47
United States
    Commission on Civil Rights (1970), 78
    Congress, 13-14
    Constitution, 49
    federal government, 51
    immigration policy, 16, 18
    Labor Department, 68
    population statistics, 3, 12
    Supreme Court, 14, 42, 49
Universal Declaration of Human Rights, 57
upward mobility, 170
vagrancy laws, 51
Voices Project, 159, 177
voting rights, 55, 58
war on drugs, 62
    drug-related funding, 60
    under Nixon, 57, 60
    under Reagan, 60-62
wealth, 78

white, 13, 24
   flight, 77
   normative standard,
     20-21, 24
   poor, 88

   supremacy, 19-22, 38, 49
   Southerners, 58
Wolterstorff, Nicholas,
   108-9
World War I, 36

World War II, 16, 56, 125,
   149, 181
Wycliffe, John, 117
Zimmerman, George,
   146-47

ABOUT THE AUTHOR

KEN WYTSMA IS A LEADER, innovator, and social entrepreneur. His work takes him around the world as a frequent international speaker on justice, theology, and leadership. Ken is known for his depth of insight and ability to inspire others to think deeply about faith, life, and leadership. *Publishers Weekly* called Ken "one of the new breed of evangelical Christians returning to scripture to redeem justice as a central tenet of faith."

Ken is the founder of The Justice Conference, an annual international conference that introduces people to a wide range of organizations and conversations related to biblical justice, which has reached over twenty thousand people at conferences across five continents.

In addition to serving as the founding pastor of Antioch Church, Ken is president of Kilns College, where he teaches courses on philosophy, justice, and creative leadership. Ken also served for several years as the executive director of a creative office for World Relief and has experience as a senior partner for a brand strategy and marketing firm.

Ken is the author of *Pursuing Justice*, *The Grand Paradox*, and *Create vs. Copy*. He has written widely, with articles appearing in *Relevant* magazine, *Huffington Post*, *Church Leaders*, *Worship Magazine*, and more. Ken lives in Bend, Oregon, with his wife, Tamara, and their four daughters.

To contact Ken about speaking
at your event, school, or
church, or to inquire about
creative consulting for your
organization, visit

kenwytsma.com

Follow Ken at:

 @kjwytsma   f @kjwytsma   🐦 @kjwytsma

Photo by Kim Landy